PRAISE FOR
Obsessive-Compulsive Disorder:
New Help for the Family

To my knowledge, there are no similar books written for family members suffering the effects of having OCD in the family. We receive hundreds of calls each year from unhappy, frustrated family members seeking ways to help the individual refusing treatment or not responding well to treatment. We will look forward to being able to refer these callers to your book.

—*Bette Hartley, M.L.S., Information Specialist, Obsessive-Compulsive Information Center*

—⟋⟍⟍—

"Trauma (is) a crucible for developing excellence...through which we turn life's wounds into gifts." Sustaining that positive note throughout, Gravitz offers a guidebook for the families of those suffering from obsessive-compulsive disorder (OCD), a book as poetical as it is practical.

A licensed psychologist experienced in dealing with families of alcoholics, Gravitz believes that families of people with OCD are too often overlooked in the treatment. His extensive experience with homes in crisis enables Gravitz to anticipate the questions, feelings and problems encountered by the OCD family. Yet, as specific as it is to this disorder, one in which fearful and repetitive thought rule a person's life, the book would be helpful to any family afflicted by chronic illness or to professionals interested in a concise, informative and highly readable text.

Gravitz' desire to educate and encourage is reflected in every aspect of the book—from organization to style. The eight chapters are arranged in a question-and-answer format for convenience; even the footnotes are in "unobtrusive superscript" to accommodate both readers and researchers. Chapters are packed with useful information, providing details about the disease as well as support for those undertaking the journey toward recovery. The book's final chapter offers practical steps and recommended routes (from setting boundaries to setting appointments with therapists) for family members to put into practice.

—*Judy Hopkins, Foreward Magazine*

—⟋⟍⟍—

In my many years of facilitating support groups and OCD information lines, many family members and loved ones ask what they can do to better the lives of the OCD sufferer. Often I tell them that they should help themselves first. I had never been able to offer such a wonderful way to start this journey prior to this book. Once you start to read the book, you begin to find that Dr. Gravitz has not only a keen understanding of Obsessive-Compulsive disorder, but also a unique compassion for the sufferer and all of those affected by this illness.

The techniques that Dr. Gravitz uses can help all impacted by the illness learn methods to cope with OCD and life in general. Anyone suffering from any chronic illness, be it OCD or not, can benefit from its techniques. I highly recommend *Obsessive-Compulsive Disorder: New Help for the Family* to all loved ones of OCD sufferers, those with the illness, or to anyone who needs to learn better of becoming a closer family unit in the midst of any chronic illness.

—Janis McClure, Former President,
Obsessive-Compulsive Foundation of Jacksonville, Florida

—⚒—

I...was delightfully caught up in the insight Herb has toward OCD and the dynamics of how the family may interact with the symptoms—couldn't put the book down. What a respectful view of OCD as a disorder and the persons as a loved one, not an object. I have recommended this book to many people and will continue to do so.

—Lorre Mendelson, Vocational Services Specialist and
expert in Employment Counseling and Mental Health

—⚒—

To those of you who are trying to understand your family member with OCD and need emotional support for your own difficult situation, this book is WONDERFUL!

—Wendy Mueller, OCD sufferer and parent of a child with OCD

—⚒—

This is the first book that I am aware of that deals with OCD from the family perspective. The dedication at the beginning of the book lays out Gravitz' guiding philosophy. "This book is dedicated to the many millions of family members and their loved ones who seek the healing edge between what is loving and responsible toward the OCD sufferer and what is loving and responsible toward themselves."

I highly recommend this book for families that have not yet found the magic bullet which keeps OCD at bay and must struggle every day with the question of what role they should play in relation to the OCD sufferer. This is a book that doesn't pretend to have all the answers, but, nevertheless, gives lots of practical advice which I think is right on target. It answers such practical questions as, "How do you respond to the OCD sufferer when he or she is in the midst of an obsession or compulsion?" "How involved should you be in your loved one's life?" "How do you deal with your loved one's bizarre behavior?" "Why do you need to take care of yourself first?"

—Pathways

You have done an excellent job in reaching out to the family members and providing them with a systematic process for dealing with OCD in the family. (Too often the families of OCD sufferers are an afterthought in treatment and little attention is paid to either their own stress and suffering or to the important role they may play in facilitating a positive treatment response.) I think your book will be extremely helpful to these families, and I look forward to using it in our treatment program at UCLA.

—John Piacentini, Ph.D., Director, Child and Adolescent OCD and Related Disorders
Program UCLA-Neuropsychiatric Institute

Dr. Gravitz' book fills a critical gap in the literature on OCD. At long last, there is a book specifically for the other victims of OCD, the families of those who suffer from this disabling disorder.

—C. Alec Pollard, Ph.D., Director, Anxiety Disorders Center,
St. Louis Behavioral Medicine Institute

New Help for the Family is like sitting in front of the fireplace on a winter's day sharing a cozy couch with your favorite uncle. Herb Gravitz extrapolates an experienced and gentle history of teaching and treating persons in trauma into an approach for the family in recovery from OCD. A blend of Jung, the Twelve Steps, a touch of Eastern philosophy and a good dose of cognitive-behavioral therapy, *Obsessive-Compulsive Disorder: New Help for the Family* is an educational, spiritual, and behavioral treat.

—Diane Sands, President & CEO,
Obsessive-Compulsive & Spectrum Disorders Association

—∿—

I love the tone of the book. It is very readable, supportive, and non-judgmental. And as a parent who lives with OCD day in and day out, I found the advice very much on the mark. Thanks for writing such a well thought out and compassionate book.

—Janet Susin, NAMI Queens/Nassau and parent of a child with OCD

—∿—

Finally! A book that deals with the impact OCD has on the family. Dr. Gravitz' quotes ring true and are thought-provoking. His down-to-earth advice is an important survival guide for those who live with someone with OCD. He gives the "para-OCD," the person who lives with the person with OCD, practical advice. Many families disintegrate along with the progression of OCD. This book offers skill and hope not only to keep the family together but to strengthen each family member.

—Fran Sydney, Board of Directors, OC Foundation, OC Newsletter, June 1998

—∿—

A pioneering work that addresses the needs of OCD caregivers. No longer is it necessary for families to surrender to OCD, to give up their freedom. Herbert Gravitz gives hope to family members and offers clear, concise ways to promote healing during OCD crises. As an OCD caregiver I am excited by this work because I will be able to use it to weaken the influence of the OCD monster in my life.

—Chris Vertullo, parent of a person with OCD and owner of OCD-L,
a discussion forum on the Internet

—∿—

Second Edition

OBSESSIVE-COMPULSIVE DISORDER

New Help for the Family

Herbert L. Gravitz, Ph.D.

With the original Foreword by James W. Broatch
Former Executive Director, OC Foundation

Healing Visions Press
Santa Barbara, California

OBSESSIVE-COMPULSIVE DISORDER
New Help for the Family

By Herbert L. Gravitz, Ph.D.

Healing Visions Press, Santa Barbara, California
www.HealTheFamily.com

ISBN 13: 978-096611047-0   ISBN 10: 0-96611047-1
LCCN 2005935981

Publisher's Cataloging-in-Publications
(Provided by *Quality Books, Inc.*)

Gravitz, Herbert L., 1942-
    Obsessive-compulsive disorder : new help for the family /
Herbert L. Gravitz. - 2nd ed.
    p. cm.
    Includes bibliographical references.
    ISBN-13: 978-096611047-0
    ISBN-10: 096611047-1
    1. Obsessive-compulsive disorder. 2. Mentally ill—Family
relationships. 3. Family psychotherapy.   I. Title. II. Title: Obsessive-
compulsive disorder
    RC533.G73 1998   616.85'227
                                          QBI98-114

Cover and book design by
Peri Poloni, Knockout Design, www.knockoutbooks.com

Dedication

—◊◊—

To the millions of family members and loved ones who seek the healing edge between what is loving and responsible toward the OCD sufferer and what is loving and responsible toward themselves.

May each of you find and unwrap the many gifts that are cloaked in your special situation, and may you see the underlying order in the midst of your apparent chaos.

With a vision, all is possible.

Other Books by Herbert L. Gravitz

Trauma and Adversity: Triumph's Crucible (Forthcoming Publication).
Santa Barbara, California: Healing Visions Press, 2006.

Mental Illness and the Family: Unlocking the Doors to Triumph.
Santa Barbara, California: Healing Visions Press, 2004.

Facing Adversity: Words That Heal.
Santa Barbara, California: Healing Visions Press, 2004.

Genesis: Spirituality in Recovery from Childhood Traumas (with J. Bowden).
Pompano Beach, Florida: Health Communications, Inc., 1988.

Recovery: A Guide for Adult Children of Alcoholics (with J. Bowden).
New York, New York: Simon and Schuster, 1987.

Contents

—⁓—

CHAPTER 4: **Identifying Your Issues—**
The Fallout of Living Under the Influence of OCD   51

CHAPTER 7: Healing the Family—
From Invisible Survivor to Visible Healer 117

—w—

Foreword

—៣—

Obsessive-Compulsive Disorder (OCD) is a family illness. This fact is a relatively new concept to most in the OCD community. However, research has consistently revealed that more than 90 percent of family members of individuals with OCD subvert their personal and family needs to accommodate their loved one's OCD symptoms. The results can be devastating! A 1993 Obsessive-Compulsive Foundation/ Fordham University study of the impact of OCD on the family broadcasts the truth: more than 80 percent of respondents noted disruption of the personal life of a family member, three-quarters of the families were disturbed by the loss of interpersonal relationships and reported marital difficulties as a result of OCD in the family. The survey also elicited what most families needed: how to respond to and cope with difficult OC behaviors.

Finally, almost four years later, Dr. Gravitz has responded with a hope-filled, down-to-earth, compassionate book that instructs families how to solve the ever-present dilemma of "trying to figure out the rightness of one's actions." Dr. Gravitz utilizes his extensive work with families of alcoholics to help families break out of the entanglement of OCD and chart a purposeful path to recovery.

His suggestions are presented in an easy-to-read question and answer format. Question: "Can I change the OCD?" Answer: "No, however you can change yourself and your reaction to this disorder." Dr. Gravitz wisely cautions his reader "Take what is helpful and leave the rest."

My prayers and thoughts are with you and your family as you embark upon your "journey of hope."

Godspeed,

James W. Broatch
Former Executive Director, OC Foundation

—〰—

Preface to the 2005 Edition

It has been more than seven years since I wrote *Obsessive-Compulsive Disorder: New Help for the Family.* Little could I have known what would unfold during those years. Little could I have foreseen all the twists and turns my own life would take, let alone the lives of my family. And little could I have grasped the plight of families firsthand until my own life changed dramatically and unexpectedly.

During these seven years, I spent more than 3,500 hours working intensively with families in my office. In addition, I lectured both in and out of my home state of California. I also consulted by telephone and e-mail with family members who had become familiar with my work. I wrote two more books and contributed articles to organizations and journals.

I realized even more how much the family matters. I re-discovered how essential the family is to each of its members by observing how poorly family members fare when their family is not working. It does not matter whether members are separated by time, space, or distance nor whether the family has stature, wealth, and opportunity. I discovered a family shouldn't stop being a family unless it is physically dangerous and life threatening.

I began to discover how to see the many resources and strengths in even the worst of families and how crucial these often unseen—and therefore untapped and unavailable—resources are to the healing process of the family and its individual members. I came to realize there is a continuum of family healing. It starts with surviving the illness, addiction, and trauma (not everyone does). It moves to members picking up the pieces, unfortunately by taking unnecessary or excessive responsibility or trying to manage ill family members through control or brute force. It continues to members becoming resilient and ultimately to members triumphing over the adversity.

Initially, I saw family resilience as a therapeutic goal and didn't distinguish resilience from triumph. I began to realize that resilience could actually hold the family back because it often stresses stability over growth. Resilience is the ability to bounce back after a setback and regain a sense of equilibrium. Triumph is the ability to bounce forward after adversity, emerging with more wisdom, patience, and skill than before. I saw how resilience could be a hindrance, a form of enabling that keeps the family returning again and again to an unhealthy balance of unworkable rules and roles that disables the family.

One reason for my concern with resilience as a treatment goal is that over time, family members develop "tolerance." Tolerance is a term from the addiction field and refers to the addicted person needing more and more of a drug to achieve less and less of an effect. In the context of family healing, tolerance refers to a form of adaptation in which family members have an increasing forbearance, or tolerance, for inappropriate behaviors. It is as if the family gets used to the strange and aberrant behaviors of their loved one.

This high tolerance works subtly as family members learn to put up with more and more behaviors that don't work. It's like the story of the frog. If I put it in boiling water, the frog would immediately jump out and escape. If I put the frog in water that gradually increases in temperature until it reaches its boiling point, the frog will get used to the water, stay, and perish.

Eventually, tolerance and adapting to inappropriate behaviors can disable everyone in the family. Tolerance is a highly maladaptive form of coping, in that it holds the whole family in a state of no-growth or stasis. Its power lies in its invisibility. As it is exposed, it is often transformed.

An example of tolerance occurred in the family who has a member with severe cleaning obsessions and rituals. At first, the compulsions were confined to the primary sufferer and didn't involve anyone else or require anyone's participation. But soon he began to ask other family members to wash their hands. Then, he insisted they take off their shoes and wash their feet in special water before entering the house. After a time during which others adapted and became used to this dysfunctional behavior, he flew into a rage if others did not take off their clothes and shower before they entered the house. Before knowing it, the family was engulfed in his OCD and couldn't remember how things got so bad.

I witnessed family members continually get caught in the exaggerations and distortions of ill members. Family members become fixated and stuck, seeing and hearing limited and distorted parts of their experience, while excluding important elements of the experience. I learned that the way through the family maze of illness, addiction, and trauma is often surprisingly simple or basic when the appropriate counsel is provided. It is, however, not at all easy.

The principles of healing are not complicated to comprehend; they are just difficult to put into action. The challenge is that this journey always begins with you. This requires your time, attention, and commitments, as well as the ability to get up one more time than you fall down.

As I look back over these years, I appreciate foremost the privilege of working with many families. Some were affected by OCD, and others were under the influence of bipolar disorder, schizophrenia, and major depression. Still others faced major adversities such as physical illness, alcoholism or other addictions.

Like the families with whom I have worked, I've had to face my own battles. I have dealt with illness, addiction, and trauma. As I was finishing the OCD book, suddenly I became the patient in my family. I was diagnosed with cancer. My family and I would soon enter a strange new world of doctors, hospitals, blood tests, body scans, insurance problems, and the overwhelming feeling that we (especially me) just weren't doing enough.

I was now the primary sufferer, the person with the illness, and my family became the secondary sufferers. They watched me as I rejected traditional medical treatment and sought primarily a spiritual path. They looked on in dismay and helplessness while I denied the seriousness of my illness and acted out the addiction to my work. My family was in the bind of seeing me falter personally, while growing professionally. By pursuing my dream of helping other families, my family was experiencing the loss of me. I was in deep trouble and I didn't notice. My family members did and didn't know what to do.

In addition, I soon realized that I most likely had an addiction to my work, although it was never formally diagnosed. Both of these adversities led my family and me down the same slippery slope of trauma that I was seeing with clients in my office and describing in my writings. Adversity forced me to look at issues that I had never looked at before. The old saying that we teach what we need to learn certainly was true for me.

In my work with families, I consistently find that the prognosis for a family and its members under the influence of commanding adversities is better when the primary sufferer has some understanding of his or her plight and surrenders to the wisdom and counsel of the other family members. I was simply unavailable to my family for any conversation about the cancer that differed from my stubborn view. Reality, however, has no respect for denial. The cancer continued to grow until the pain of the tumors shattered my denial, and I received the appropriate treatment.

Typically, my wife would accompany me for treatment. Soon she would leave an appointment feeling invisible because the toll on her was given lip service at best. At worst, she was subtly blamed for not helping me more. The rest of my family was seen as a peripheral part of my healing, yet these "neglected affected" were the people that I loved and with whom I spent the most time. When it is my time to die, I will not count the number of books I wrote but the number of loving moments I shared.

From this bittersweet process, together with the lessons from working with other families, I now see additional important patterns that underlie family and individual healing. Perhaps the most liberating is the discovery that the primary sufferer does not have to get better for other members in the family to get better. I learned that it is never too late for family members to have full, meaningful lives if they dare. From this process also, I wanted to share through my writing what I was learning with other families and the professionals who treat them.

The original edition of *Obsessive-Compulsive Disorder* was the first book in what forms a trilogy on the impact of serious mental illness and other adversities (SMIA) on the individual and the family. Each of the next two books addresses this impact and describes the family and individual healing process from a different vantage point. The purpose of this educational trilogy is to help family members become aware through thought, word, and deed that they can have a more fulfilling, empowered life.

My first effort to describe how a family deals with mental illness was very specific: an illness called obsessive-compulsive disorder or OCD. The second, *Mental Illness and the Family: Unlocking the Doors to Triumph,* was more general in scope. I wrote about the possibility of thriving in the midst of any mental illness, or, by inference, any situation or event that is overwhelming. The third book, *Facing Adversity: Words That Heal,* is a compendium of words attributed to some of the greatest healers of all time, and gently guides the reader through the stages of individual and family recovery. It completes this trilogy by revealing the universality of our wounding and shows that adversity is inevitable. Although the books comprise an interrelated series, each book is complete on its own.

In this new edition of *Obsessive-Compulsive Disorder,* I have sharpened my focus, which has added clarity and depth to the original book. My thinking remains consistent, but it has developed and expanded enormously. All three books expound upon what I've learned about families and present a coherent picture of the family and the individual healing process. They can be read separately or as a group of related works.

Most importantly, I have learned, not by reading in my library or by writing at my computer, but in my consultation room facing families as they struggled under the daily burdens of serious adversity. And I have learned as my family and I have struggled with our own adversities. Some families with whom I have worked are intact families; others are not. Some are single-generation families; many are families spanning three generations. I am blessed by grace and age to work with a four-generation family, starting with the grandfather and including the great-grandchildren, even though the latter are too young to come to my office (other than to be breast-fed).

By observing the behaviors of the different generations sitting in my consultation room, I am able to observe the intergenerational transmission. I grasp how the sins (e.g., the dysfunctions) of the father (and mother) can be passed on to the children in the sense that they learn the repetitive negative patterns of their parents. I see these generational patterns enacted in front of me when the children repeat the same dysfunctional issues as the parents.

To expand awareness of the depth of problems incurred by illness, addiction, and trauma, I have searched outside the traditional bounds of psychiatry and psychology. I have employed more than a dozen different fields in this trilogy to understand the wounds that all members incur and to apply this knowledge to the process of family healing. Some areas of study include traumatic stress, addiction, altered states of consciousness, mythology, spirituality, loss and grieving, physical healing, personal success and happiness, neuroscience, and the new sciences.

The most basic principle that I learned is that the healthiest and hardiest among us are usually those who are embedded in a structure where members are able to work together throughout their lives, call upon one another, remember one another, gather at emergencies, celebrate life's joys, and console each other about life's miseries. When this bonding and connection does not occur, whether because of illness, addiction, or trauma, family members fall under the deep trance, or spell, of SMIA. This concept, developed fully in *Mental Illness and the Family* proves to be invaluable to family members, helping them to break the trance that binds them in dysfunctional ways.

As family members are drawn into their loved one's adversity, they can develop a parallel disorder that affects those who are most intimately involved with the primary sufferer. Whenever illness, addiction, or trauma strikes the family (and they frequently occur together, or are "co-morbid"), everyone is affected, some more than others. It is impossible to escape the effects if one is a caring and sensitive human being.

This should not be a surprise. All members of the family are joined together at the hip, regardless of the kind of relationship and regardless of how distant or how long it has been since members have seen each other. We are programmed by evolution, "wired" if you will, to need family to survive. When the family works well, its members become interdependent and need each other. To call this "codependence" misses the point that the family's reaction in the presence of great adversity is natural and predictable. Because the family is not helped, it often does the wrong things for the right reasons, namely for the well-being of the ill person.

As explained in *Mental Illness and the Family,* the transmission of this parallel disorder is called secondary traumatization or vicarious traumatization. It is more commonly referred to as "witness trauma," compassion fatigue, learned helplessness, and burnout. These can be confused with codependency. Such a disorder always comes through intimate exposure to the trauma, stress, loss, grief, and the inevitable exhaustion that family members experience as they try to deal with the hardships of their loved ones. Their job is often 24/7, which leaves little time for members to develop themselves.

In this way, SMIA reaches beyond its immediate and apparent effects and becomes a family affair. The family's resulting demoralization can be as devastating as the adversity itself. Initially, family members may be unaware of the impact on them. Like the primary sufferer, they may not want to face the reality of their situation. Their denial and minimization becomes a hallmark in a similar way, as denial and minimization are often hallmarks of SMIA. Such defenses seemingly protect members from the terror of acknowledging that their lives are out of control. The family is no longer a safe place in which to communicate, to grow, or to love. Implicit rules guide the family along a path of sickness and, at times, destruction. Members begin to develop ways of coping with family life that simply do not work.

We can look at the family plight in many ways. The well-known Chinese ideogram for crisis is composed of two symbols: danger and opportunity. To the degree that the adversity triggers members to open their eyes to a greater purpose, to a larger reality than the confines of trauma, and to a more transcendent outlook on life, the more meaningful and satisfying a life family members will have. What is more common is that the family is blamed and punished rather than seen as having an opportunity to be initiated into a higher level of consciousness in the mythic sense of the "dark night of the soul." Rather than being praised for its commitment and courage, it is often forced into hiding by clouding it in shame. There is still much stigma associated with mental illness in particular and wounding in general.

It has just been in recent decades that the family has been seen as optional. Only in this throwaway, dispensable culture do we seek to dispense with the family. It is our oldest and most sacred institution. And it may be the only place where we cannot be replaced. Yet, somehow it has become wrong to honor and protect the sanctity of the family and to fight for it against cultural forces that can pathologize it with perjorative and negative labels or terms like codependence and victimization. Even the term "survivor" might not capture the valor of many of today's families who actually triumph and thrive, not in spite of the problem but because of it.

Those who do not have an adequate understanding of their situation endure inordinate and unnecessary suffering, a type of pain that is unending and irresolvable. By experiencing the pain inherent in the situation, as opposed to suffering, family members can move forward and stop repeating the endless patterns that accompany suffering. Many family members manage both their pain and suffering by getting appropriate information, education, and support from a variety of sources (for a list of some of these sources, see this book as well as *Mental Illness and the Family: Unlocking the Doors to Triumph* and *Facing Adversity: Words That Heal*). Some are fortunate to come under the care of a knowledgeable professional.

In my work with families, I have learned that no matter how large or small the number of family members present in my office, whenever I spoke, it affected other family members who might not have been there to hear directly. I realized that my words might somehow reach all members. My experience has borne this out. I witnessed an entrainment process in the family, much like the physicists describe, akin to the synchronization of clocks with pendulums when placed together, or the regularity of the menstrual cycle with women who live together.

It is critical for families to know that relapses in the symptoms of the primary sufferer and secondary sufferers are normal and to be expected. Expectations must be constantly monitored and reassessed as family healing progresses. Because family healing is typically a lifelong journey, members should know that it is to be expected that they may want to quit at various junctures along the way. This, too, is normal.

I have learned to follow still other key principles as I work with families, regardless of diagnosis or severity. The principles contribute to family healing, which is distinct from family therapy. In the former, there is a facilitator who knows how to elicit the resources already present in each member of the family, even those not formerly seen. In the latter, there is a therapist, who directs the family treatment and diagnoses what is wrong.

This emphasis to treat what is wrong with the family is distinct from the emphasis to focus on what it is doing right and building an empowered family from there. Unless the family is severely damaged, it is almost always doing one more thing right than wrong, even if this is hard to see. A family member, for example, who refuses to come in for help but doesn't sabotage the family healing process can be acknowledged for his or her independence, and this can be used as a bridge to get the person to participate. When this family member observes how well others are doing, the person is now more likely to shift positions and take part in the healing process. A critical role of the professional helper is to find the one more thing right that family members are doing and keep mirroring it back to them, so the family has the energy, strength, and hope to do better and to know that they have more resources than ever imagined—they just must be found and utilized.

Another brief example can illustrate this critical point. The Smith family made an appointment because they "wanted to be ready" when their 16-year-old son returned from a treatment center for OCD. They had been "in therapy" many times before, but each time the father would quit because "nothing was happening except me being blamed for everything."

When I met with the family, the father again was quickly criticized as the one who was "resistant" to treatment and who sabotaged prior treatment efforts. I began to point out all the ways that the father was being "flexible." There he was in my office attending a family healing session and listening to what I had to say! "That's flexibility in action," I said. And with each example to the family of how flexible he was, the father became a little more flexible. Feeling acknowledged, perhaps for the first time, he could now use his abilities and strengths—not to defend himself as he had done before, but to engage in new behaviors and express buried feelings.

This father kept stepping in the same trap—trying to control everyone else in the family "for their own good." He kept impaling himself on the same hook of control, but he learned to stop controlling others more and more quickly. At an opportune time, I shared the following joke with him about two fish swimming in a pond. One fish said to the other, "Look at that fish. He has gotten hooked five times and each time it has gotten off the hook—he's great." But the older, wiser fish said, "Yes, but look at this magnificent one. He hasn't gotten hooked once."

Confusing control for power, families often must make decisions for their ill family member that disempower the loved one. They sacrifice long-term gain for short-term pain. Whenever I ask family members to make a decision regarding their loved ones, I ask them to go into the future and consider the impact of their decision a week from now, a month from now, a year from now, five years from now, fifteen years, and thirty years from now. Simply asking a question such as this re-orients family members and invites them to experience a bigger perspective. I've heard that some Native American elders consider the impact of every major decision they make for seven generations.

What I have also learned by listening to families and to myself is the critical distinction between "caretaking" and "caregiving." *Mental Illness and the Family* explains the subtleties between these two deceptively similar "coping" strategies. Caretaking involves giving in to another in order to prove your value or giving in to another in order to be accepted. Caregiving is providing for another so that both of you can grow and mature. There is a mutuality of learning in caregiving. There is a give and take to the process. Caretaking is a win-lose or lose-lose situation, while caregiving is a win-win situation. Caregiving is an act of interdependence, while caretaking is an act without mutuality or reciprocity. Caretaking usually engenders additional impairment in the primary as well as the secondary sufferers; caregiving facilitates recovery in both.

Nearly all family members start out as caretakers and most can learn to become caregivers. This arduous and triumphant journey is described in greater detail in my three books. This is the journey or "family odyssey," one in which each member, to the best of his or her abilities, learns the difference between a "sacred wound" and a "profane wound." This key distinction gives members a powerful tool to interpret each moment of their life as meaningful or not meaningful. Scientific research shows again and again that a meaningful life is highly correlated with a "full life," one that includes the enjoyment of physical pleasures and the use of the person's talents in productive ways. A full life is relatively independent of external events; therefore, almost all members can attain it if they make the trek.

Another step in the healing process is to discover how the family can become modern-day heroes rather than victims of an outside force. The hero or heroine surrenders to the inevitability of pain and suffering. The hero doesn't blame others or situations but instead takes responsibility for himself or herself. In a sense, heroes learn to "do within" while "doing without," having developed a strong sense of purpose and meaning in lives that sustain them. Heroes know that detaching from the dysfunction of their loved ones, not their loved ones, is the task, and often a Herculean task.

Heroes are willing to make the tough decisions in the family, decisions that increasingly place more and more appropriate responsibility on the ill member—in fact, on all members. Learning heroic action takes time. It is like paying a mortgage—the first twenty years is all interest; it is the last ten years when the equity accrues. Heroes know that life is a marathon, not a sprint. Again these concepts are discussed in detail in *Mental Illness and the Family* as well as *Facing Adversity*.

Heroes hold as a possibility that good things can come from bad circumstances. Imagine that you have just gotten married and you are spending your honeymoon in a rustic cabin in the forest. Every morning at dawn a woodpecker starts pecking away on the roof of your cabin and awakens you. How might you react? This is a true story of a young couple on their honeymoon. They are Gracie and Walter Lanz. A noisy woodpecker that disturbed them every morning led them to create the well-known cartoon character Woody the Woodpecker. Many years later, when asked about the incident with the woodpecker, Gracie said, "It was the best thing that ever happened to us."

To accomplish all of these very learnable qualities, the family must learn to become a "living family healing center" for its member—all of its members. Family members, especially children, are not easy to ignore. So the family must establish a healing center, an experiential learning community, to surround all members with the reality of their behavior so everyone has the opportunity to learn to become more responsible and capable.

With a family healing center, problems are acknowledged, there is open and direct communication among the members, there are no secrets, there is mutual tolerance and respect for all members, and members demonstrate ongoing caring for, commitment to, and affection for each other. There is a family-centered locus of all problems; individuals aren't blamed and members engage in solution-oriented problem solving together whenever possible. There is no physical violence or its threat, emotional violence is kept to a minimum, and there is no active chemical dependence.

Denial and minimization fuel adversity, while straight talk fuels healing, disables enabling, and promotes responsibility by all members of the family. Professional counseling is needed when the family cannot do these processes on its own. Major trauma and adversity often necessitate outside help. The goal of this type of family healing through a living family healing center is the attainment of the qualities described throughout this Preface.

A very different outcome occurred when thousands of ill family members were sent home to their families of origin, families who neither were taught how to respond nor were supported in their attempts. This actually happened to families in the 1960s, especially in California, where a "deinstitutionalization" movement to free psychiatric patients eliminated nine out of ten psychiatric hospital beds in a single generation. In effect, the family was forced to become a treatment center, only one that was never trained—but often blamed. Nor was the family often seen as the resource it could be when it was working well.

This new family healing center model teaches the concepts of family strength and resources. It stresses that the family is as strong as its strongest member and that members fall into deep family trances rather than being pathological. It leads members on the journey they must take to face their demons and dispel dysfunctional myths.

In the healing process, family members learn to expand and enlarge their explanations of what is happening into a great and new story. The small, old story shrinks, and the process culminates in a family becoming a home-based healing center where each member, according to ability, makes responsible choices that can work for everyone. Problems are now seen as sand for the family's oyster, not as sources of rebuke for what they did or did not do. Every family is different and creates its own story, or explanation, of what has happened.

The defining characteristic of such a healing environment is the authenticity of the family members. What creates the opportunity for true healing is the ability and willingness of each family member to be who he or she is. It is to have a voice. It is to experience and talk about what each person sees, hears, feels, senses, and knows. In this atmosphere, each person is immersed in what they are doing that works and what they are doing that doesn't work. There is ongoing feedback as to the consequences of each person's behavior on others. Such an environment offers the possibility to rise above the noise and not fall into the drama of the circumstance.

So, with this Preface to the current edition of *Obsessive-Compulsive Disorder: New Help for the Family,* I invite you, my reader, to join me on a family healing journey, which begins with you. It is a journey from what might be the specifics of your problem, to the general aspects of your life, and to the universality of your situation. It is important to remember that the family under the influence of illness, addiction, and trauma reflects a wider reality that is occurring collectively. For better and for worse, illness, addiction, and trauma require the best of us and often offer human growth and transformation in return. You'll find updated resources for information and support to help with the journey listed in Appendix A.

In conclusion, this trilogy—*Obsessive-Compulsive Disorder: New Help for the Family, Mental Illness and the Family: Unlocking the Doors to Triumph,* and *Facing Adversity: Words That Heal*—is a celebration of the human spirit and the ability not only to survive heart-wrenching adversity, but to thrive in virtually any circumstance. If people like Viktor Frankl, Mahatma Gandhi, and Nelson Mandela can achieve "thrivorship" despite horrific circumstances, then you and I have the possibility, too. It's more important than ever in our post-9-11 climate that we do so. The time is now. Let us begin.

March 13, 2005
Santa Barbara, California

—✺—

Acknowledgments

—⚭—

No book is the product of one person. This book is no exception. First and foremost, I would like to thank the first family under the influence of OCD with whom I had the privilege to work. Unfortunately, I cannot thank them by name because there is still much shame and stigma attached to this illness. Yet, without them this book could not have been written nor would I have been enriched by sharing their experience.

Second, I would like to acknowledge Meredith Boyd, the absolute best administrative assistant, research assistant, publicist, and all around "person Friday" that an author could wish for. Without her invaluable contribution, this book would not have been completed as easily and as quickly. Each and every time, Meredith did much more than I expected. Each and every time, Meredith exceeded every wish I had. From the first word of the manuscript to the final book in your hand, Meredith's gifted presence guided every phase of the book. I can never thank her enough!

Although I assume full responsibility for all errors, numerous people generously contributed time, effort, and attention to the completion of this book. In alphabetical order, they include the following:

Frances Anne (Annie) Boyd for her great heart, eagle-eye editing, and fine-tuning throughout all of the revisions.

James Callner for his undiluted enthusiasm, encouragement, humor, wit, and welcoming friendship. I look forward to the future!

Rex Dickens, author and pioneer in the impact of mental illness on siblings and offspring, whose careful editing and helpful suggestions made this a more readable book, and whose warm friendship is a treasure found.

Jay Fruehling, M.A., Information Specialist at the University of Wisconsin-Madison Medical School, for his insightful, thorough, and thought-provoking comments and suggestions.

Ellen Harper, D.D.S, M.A., whose keen insight, critical eye, and red pen made this book a much clearer and more readable text. Her contribution to the first draft was considerable. Her friendship is even more considerable.

Bette Hartley, M.L.S., of the Obsessive-Compulsive Information Center, for her skillful comments, and her constant source of useful, up-to-date information that contributed immensely to the accuracy of this book.

Judy Leach for her encouragement, support, and timely comments.

Donna Mayeux, M.A., and Joyce Burland, Ph.D., for their pioneering work with families and their encouragement to me. Donna was especially helpful in providing information on the Journey of Hope.

Kate Neiswander for her invaluable suggestions about order and sequence.

John Piacentini, Ph.D., for his encouragement and his willingness to endorse the book and incorporate it into the UCLA Child and Adolescent Program.

Roy C. for his initial encouragement, generosity, and willingness to make comments on the manuscript at its various stages.

Diane Sands, President/CEO, Obsessive-Compulsive and Spectrum Disorders Association, for her early faith in my work and her helpful suggestions.

Gail Kearns for her proofreading of the final manuscript.

Chris Vertullo, Ph.D., for her helpful comments, especially about online-computer assistance.

Gerry Wilcove, Ph.D., for his insightful comments.

And Raymond Wilcove, whose insight and acumen have made this book a better work, just as they have in all the other books he has edited for me.

A very special thank you to Jim Broatch, former Executive Director of the Obsessive-Compulsive Foundation, for his faith in my early work on the impact of OCD upon the family and for his willingness to write the Foreword to this book.

Special thanks, again in alphabetical order, go to the following:

Anne Brode, body worker extraordinaire, whose early faith created light and whose skill kept my back well during the arduous process of writing.

Breck Costin, master motivator, seminar leader, and consultant. While his influence on this particular writing is not obvious, his overall influence on my development, maturity, and leadership is immeasurable.

Ralph Daniel, Ph.D., whose friendship, support, and sound judgment are treasures.

Barbara Deutsch for her overall razor-sharp counsel and wisdom.

Andrea Dominic-Hoyt, whose closing counsel offered the possibility of a new beginning.

Federico Grosso, D.D.S, Ph.D., M.F.C.C., dearest friend, trusted colleague, and one of the most gifted and creative therapists that I have had the privilege to know.

Peter J. Levy, D.C., healer, and one of the best friends a man can have.

Stephen McEachen, Ph.D., whose initial assistance was essential to this project.

Coral Markle, one of my true heroes and a living testimony to the journey from trauma to excellence.

Deborah Ross, Ph.D., therapist extraordinaire, whose "rest home for weary therapists" in Los Gatos, California, was an early retreat for me. I will always treasure her faith in me and the valuable lessons she taught.

Gerald Tarlow, Ph.D., behavior therapist extraordinaire, whose commitment to his patients is a model for all therapists who work with OCD.

Last but not least, I would like to thank my wife and companion of almost forty years, Leslie Ann, and my three great sons, all of whom one more time shared and endured my labor with this book. Leslie, as usual, made sure my thinking was clear, logical, and concise. Many of her suggestions were instrumental in increasing the warmth and humanity of the book. My youngest son, Mike, read and commented on many parts of the draft. I have no doubt that this resulted in a simpler, less technical book. My middle son, Aaron, was invaluable for his technical assistance with the computer, e-mail, and all those mechanical obstacles he helped me overcome. And, of course, my thanks to Brian, my first born, for his encouragement, wisdom, and good cheer. Thanks, too, to Sabra, trustworthy dog, who laid patiently at my feet and kept me company during the long hours that it took to complete this project.

—⁂—

A Note to the Family

—⚞—

Unlike other books, which have been written primarily for the person with OCD, *Obsessive-Compulsive Disorder: New Help for the Family* is for you, the family members and loved ones of someone who is suffering from OCD. It is for you, the parents, the spouses, the children, the siblings, and the friends of the person with OCD. It is for those of you who have become caught in the tangled web of OCD and have come under its far-reaching influence.

This book presents a step-by-step, practical plan of recovery. It will provide much-needed information, help, and support for those affected by what may be one of the most devastating of all psychiatric disorders. It will help you understand what is happening to you and those you love. It will tell you how to take better care of yourself and, as a result, will show you how to be more helpful to the person with OCD. Thus, this book is not just a survival manual for family members, but a guide to finding your way out of the web of OCD so that everyone affected by OCD can enjoy life again. When OCD's impact and its full treatment are understood, there are often immediate and dramatic changes in everyone.

But first, you must help yourself. Remember the last time you were on an airplane? The flight attendant announced that in the event of a loss in cabin pressure, a mask would drop to provide you with oxygen. Remember that you were directed to secure your own mask first before trying to help your child or the person next to you. The reason is painfully simple: if you lose consciousness from a lack of oxygen, you will be in no position to help anyone else. Yet every time you board an airplane you are told the same thing because in a crisis most people's first reaction is to help those they love first. While the intention may be noble, unless you are obtaining life-giving oxygen and breathing yourself, you won't be able to save anyone else, let alone yourself.

The same principle applies here as well. Taking care of yourself ensures that you will be able to support others when needed. Unless you take care of yourself and stay physically, emotionally, and spiritually healthy, you won't be able to help yourself, your family, or the person with OCD. Only when your cup is full can it run over and be shared with others.

The noted writer Robert Louis Stevenson said, "Life is not so much a matter of holding good cards, but sometimes of playing a poor hand well." We can enjoy happy and productive lives regardless of the situation in which we find ourselves. Too much attention has been given to the horrors, the sadness, and losses of OCD rather than the possibilities and the gains. During stressful circumstances we develop the fortitude that molds our character. When we experience our "dark night of the soul," there is the possibility to emerge stronger!

There is a burgeoning body of literature that provides a road map to overcoming adversity. People can recover from all kinds of injuries. Healing from malignant tumors as well as from dysfunctional and codependent relationships shows that we can recover from virtually any circumstance. Adversity, when dealt with forthrightly, develops resilience.[11,18,22,26,29,35,38,39,42,46,51,55,58]

All chronic illnesses, including OCD, are difficult. But with what we are learning about OCD, there is reason for optimism. While the tendency is still to shroud OCD in secrecy and denial, the disorder is rapidly "coming out of the closet." Healing is actually occurring, and there are more and more individuals and families who have not only recovered but have actually blossomed. OCD can become a pathway toward something greater, bigger, and more meaningful than you ever expected.[26,55]

While you have neither asked for nor wanted this relationship with OCD, the great myths that have withstood the test of time teach us that we are never pleased when we are given a major life task or given a "call." Typically, the mythic hero is reluctantly called upon to slay the dragon, find the princess, or search for the Grail. When looking at healing from the mythological viewpoint, it can be seen that you have been called to go on your own journey—your journey of selfhood from victim to hero.[10,31]

Like the Biblical miracle of parting the Red Sea, the source of the miraculous is often some catastrophe. Therefore, another powerful way to interpret or create your experience is to embrace crisis. The Chinese have an interesting way of forming the word "crisis." The word is composed of two symbols, one for danger and one for opportunity. OCD can be viewed as the juncture between danger and opportunity. When you embrace the opportunity, your wound becomes what in mythological terms is called a "sacred wound," one which opens and deepens your heart, soul, and spirit.[31]

When you view your experience or journey with OCD in this way, you will indeed maximize your ability to learn and to grow. It is my personal hope and my professional conviction that you, your family, and your loved ones can meet this crisis, or challenge, with knowledge, skill, love, and spirit. I fully believe that you can emerge with a stronger sense of self and family. I also believe that you and your family can find new joy and meaning in your lives.

It is not only your right—but your responsibility—to heal what may be thought of as your sacred wound, and I am honored to join you on this journey. My father always used to tell me that God gives us gifts, and they are always wrapped in problems. May this book help you unwrap the gifts in your problems.

A major purpose in writing this book will be achieved if it prompts you to examine and reflect on how to better understand the role you play in helping a loved one with OCD and how to maintain your own sense of self and purpose at the same time.

Come, let us join forces and continue....

A Special Note to the Person With OCD

—⌇⌇—

I would like to extend a special welcome to you, the person with OCD. It's good to have you aboard! You are a crucial element in family healing.

First, I acknowledge your courage and strength. To participate in the world beyond the influence of OCD requires bravery beyond measure. I understand that your view of the world is shaped by the belief that you or someone else is constantly in great, often life-threatening, danger. Not surprisingly, your feelings follow your beliefs, and you are terrified much of the time and driven by enormous fear even when you aren't directly under the influence of OCD. The old adage that seeing is believing is simply not true for you, for often you can't trust what you see—or hear. You cannot trust your own senses to give you the information you need to make daily decisions. In fact, it is your own sensory experience gone haywire that causes you so much horror, fright, confusion, and doubt. From this foreboding place, you are left to create your world. It's a tough job.

Second, I honor your commitment to your family. I know that reading this book may prove painful at times. It may evoke strong feelings of regret and guilt to read how some of your behaviors can be disruptive and hurt the very people you love the most. Yet, if you are still reading this book, it is clear that your love for your family is even stronger than your fear and guilt. Why else would you continue? I believe it's your commitment and love for your family that keeps you reading. Your curiosity is also welcomed. If you read this guide carefully, you may feel some joy as your family and loved ones move through their own healing. If they are to be the healing agents and caregivers who lovingly nurture you, they must do their own healing too.

Third, I salute your freedom. The poet Sartre once noted, "Freedom is what you do with what's been done to you." In this moment of time, here and now, you are in what I call an "OCD-free zone," or a state of mind in which the OCD isn't controlling or directing your behavior. This does not mean that you are not anxious or fearful or even that you are not obsessing or ritualizing at this very moment. It does mean, however, that at least in terms of reading this book now, you are in control of the OCD. You have the illness; the illness doesn't have you. The OCD isn't dominating you like it can when you are under its spell of obsession and compulsion.

I wish you a divinely inspired healing journey. Healing involves the development of more and more of these OCD-free zones. Developing free zones is similar to building a muscle. Most benefits come at the very end of the stretch when the fiber ruptures and the nerve registers the pain. Nature overcompensates and within forty eight hours the muscle fiber is strengthened. Your emotional muscles develop in much the same way. When you exercise discipline over OCD, your emotional muscle fiber is broken down, nature overcompensates, and next time the OCD-free zone fiber is bigger and stronger.

I invite you to join with me and your family in a journey of love and healing. Your OCD needn't stop you from creating a "win-win-win-win" experience. First, it can be a win for your family, because they are helped; second, it can be a win for your other loved ones, because they are helped; and third, it can be a win for you, because you win whenever they do. Finally, it can also be a win for you because you get something for yourself—perhaps more understanding, new and useful information, or comfort.

I will celebrate your victories, for each and every victory for you is also a victory for those you love. In turn, each victory for them is a victory for you. It's the beginning of an interdependent relationship where everyone can win and everyone becomes capable of being a caregiver, not a caretaker.

So, lastly, I wish you Godspeed on your own special journey of healing. I wish you peace, freedom, quiet, and connection to yourself, others, and the larger community. God bless....

Introduction

—⚭—

*J*im stands outside the bathroom door trying to decide what to do while Mary, his wife and mother of their two children, is bent over the bathroom sink. She is feverishly washing her hands because she believes they are contaminated. They are red, cracked, and sometimes bleed. Lost in endless repetition, she is temporarily entranced by the fear that is driving her washing, and she is oblivious to her family.

Some days are consumed with washing. On others, Mary races from one frightening thought of disaster to another. The endless washing is replaced by endless fears of injury or contamination. If Jim had the words, he might describe this familiar pattern of change as "obsession hopping." Sometimes these changes seem to come from nowhere. And equally suddenly and inexplicably, Mary is her old self again. During these times, the spell is broken...for awhile.

Jim's impatience grows as his mind rewinds and reviews his entire history with Mary. He wonders how things have become so bad. Mary wasn't always like this. Suddenly, he realizes that everyone has been waiting for what seems an eternity for Mary to go to the boys' Little League game. And one more time, she is unable to participate in the family's everyday activities.

Jim is angry because he feels like a "single" parent. But, at the same time, he also feels guilty that he hasn't been supportive enough of his wife. Once again, he is torn between his compassion for Mary and his own anger and frustration with a situation he doesn't understand. He feels helpless to change what's happening and is clueless as to how to manage it. He must make the painful decision whether to leave now and take Tommy and Sam to the game and return for Mary later or perhaps wait a little longer and hope that Mary will be able to finish her cleansing routine instead of letting down the children one more time.

Jim has loved Mary since the first day he met her, but he feels as if he has lost a big part of her to this nameless intruder. He also worries that he is neglecting his children because of his continuous preoccupation with his wife. As far as his own needs, it's been so long since he or anyone else paid attention to them, he wonders if he will ever get them met again. When Mary isn't actively engaging in her rituals and compulsions, Jim and the kids are relieved but are still worried about them starting again.

In another family, Rita and Ron have been waiting for hours for their adult son Mark to arrive for a long-planned family gathering. They are worried about what might have happened to him, but they speculate that he must have gotten trapped again in one of his numerous compulsions. They are right, unfortunately. On the way to his parents' house, Mark thought he heard a thump under his car, and he imagined that he might have run over someone. Although he knew this was unlikely, he turned around to check for signs of an accident. After checking several times, he continued on his way, only to think that he heard another thump. Consequently, he arrived hours late.

Mark began to develop strange habits as he was growing up. Even as a young child, he became obsessively concerned that he'd hurt someone. Now, as a young adult, Mark's fears and behaviors are manageable more often than not. And, since he owns his own small business, he can usually make adjustments for his lateness. Yet, because he is late so often, his business is marginal and Ron and Rita provide financial aid. "Why can't he just set aside his problems for

even a little while and enjoy the family's company for the evening?"
they wonder. "Is he crazy?"

Rita and Ron know that Mark has a problem, but they are unsure
just what is wrong. They secretly worry that they might have contributed to his strange behavior. They are afraid for their son, yet they are
also angry and frustrated. They are tired of worrying and waiting, and
they wish for just one day when their family would be normal. Most of
the time, though, they worry about what will happen to him when they
are gone or too old to supplement his limited income.

In still another family, Marissa, a cute eight-year-old, is sitting
in the back seat of the family car. She is confused and frightened as
she watches her father, Ted, dart in and out of the house. She has
seen him frantic like this many times before. She thinks back to the
day that he checked the garden hose all morning, making sure it was
tightly turned off, turning it on and turning it off again and again.
He finally stopped, and she cried when she saw his red and blistered
hands. Marissa is convinced that her dad cares more about the appliances, windows, and locks than he does about her because he spends
so much time checking them.

Marissa constantly worries about her father. His strange behavior
seems to be getting worse, and she doesn't understand what's wrong
with her daddy or what to do about it. She's ashamed to bring friends
home because her father is so strange, and she cannot count on him not
to embarrass her. Marissa secretly fears that she might become like her
dad someday, and she doesn't know who to talk to. She's tried to talk
to her mother about her worries, but her mother just gets irritated and
says, "Don't be silly." Mom appears as distraught at times as Dad, and
Marissa feels alone.

Later in the day Aunt Betty finds Marissa crying. When Marissa
tells her how scared she is, her aunt offers comfort and safety. Aunt
Betty talks with Marissa about her dad, Aunt Betty's brother, and lets
Marissa know that his behavior is indeed strange. She also tells Marissa
that it is not her fault and that she can't "catch" it from her father.
Marissa feels relieved and wishes she could live with Aunt Betty and

Uncle Bill. Later, as an adult, she will look back and remember her Aunt Betty as someone who made a difference.

In the Federico family, Eduardo and Susan are arguing again about what to do about their daughter, May. Her behavior has become increasingly unusual and disruptive. Edwardo insists that they need to be more strict with her and punish her when she gets into one of her odd routines. But Susan is convinced that reassurance is the best way to handle the problem.

Unable to resolve their differences, Eduardo and Susan search for someone to blame. Their daughter was a happy, healthy child until she was five years old and started a new school. Then she began doing strange things like arranging and rearranging her toys and stuffed animals in very strict order over and over again. She had always been a neat and tidy little girl, but now she had to get things "just right" or she couldn't leave her room.

May's parents tried to ignore these changes in her behavior. They hoped that as she became used to the new environment, her habits would subside. Instead, she got more upset and seemed almost driven. The day before her teacher called to report that their daughter—a bright girl—wasn't getting her papers completed and that it took May an unusually long time to check her answers. She was having so much difficulty that she was slowing down the class and the other children were making fun of her. May was crying more and more frequently at school, and the teacher expressed her concern and asked for Susan and Eduardo's help.

Edwardo and Susan are concerned and consumed by guilt. They worry that their frequent fights have made May's bizarre activities worse. How can they help their little girl? How can they find time and energy to devote to their other two children? They feel overwhelmed and are embarrassed.

Eduardo and Susan seek help. They search for a counselor who is familiar with behaviors such as these. When they finally locate a therapist who recognizes May's behavior patterns, he tells them that May has Obsessive-Compulsive Disorder or OCD. The therapist recommends a book about OCD and refers them to an educational group for families living with OCD. Here they learn what they can do to help May and what they must avoid doing. But just as importantly, they learn what they can do to help themselves. They are relieved to finally know how to help. For the first time they have hope because they can see May's OCD as an illness. The tension between them lessens. They begin to care for themselves and enjoy a healthier family life.

With their therapist's help, they work with May in behavior therapy. May is also placed on antidepressant medication by her therapist. Her parents attend a local self-help group meeting to get support from others living with OCD. Gradually, they notice a difference, and everyone seems to improve as OCD is no longer the central organizing factor in their lives. Every family decision is no longer funneled through the OCD. May's habits and her mind-set improve, and her parents relax their perfectionist standards at home. For Susan and Eduardo, the sense of relief about May's future and their ability to care for their other children greatly enhances their quality of life. They are no longer exhausted when their alarm goes off in the morning, and "family night out" becomes a weekly event. Susan and Edwardo's relationship improves and they recommit to their romance. There is increasing time and energy for everyone in the family.

A Surprisingly Common Plight

Scenes like these unfold everyday behind closed doors in millions of families everywhere.[50] There are many people like Mary, Mark, Ted, and May. These OCD sufferers could be your next-door neighbor or the man in the grocery line; they could be your wife, child, parent, sibling, dear friend, or other loved one. As you will see, these frightened and driven people share a common problem. They have OCD. Their loved ones, like the Jims, Rons and Ritas, and Marissas, suffer as well. They, too, are under the influence of one of the most heart-wrenching and devastating illnesses.

All these people are trying to live with Obsessive-Compulsive Disorder, which until recently was thought to be very rare. Also called the "Doubting Disease," those with OCD seem unable to trust their own senses or their intuition. They are afflicted with fearful and repetitive thoughts that drive them to perform senseless rituals in order to reduce these fearful thoughts, but they get no lasting relief from these efforts. In fact, they typically feel worse and soon start the cycle all over again.

OCD is a complex and puzzling psycho-neuro-physiological disorder.[21,32]

I believe it becomes a spiritual disorder as well because, in time, sufferers can experience a profound loss of self, analogous to the spiritual bankruptcy that alcoholics suffer. They become disconnected from self, others, and something beyond and greater than themselves.

Many professionals call OCD a disease or illness. We still don't know exactly what causes it, although we are getting some good ideas. OCD strikes the afflicted individual plus it can also affect everyone under its influence. Because there is evidence suggesting that genetics play a part in the development of OCD,[32,34] it may even be a generational illness. Regardless of the cause, OCD can be devastating to everyone within its sphere of influence. OCD can cause traumatic stress responses in both the individuals suffering from it and their family members.

The loved ones in a family under the influence of OCD often struggle with a sense of personal and familial loss. They may have suffered for years as well, not understanding why their lives were becoming increasingly difficult and unmanageable or wondering why they, too, felt anger, guilt, and despair. And like the individual sufferer, family members often become more isolated from others over time.

OCD and Trauma

I was counseling a family early in its recovery. The OCD sufferer in the family had just expressed how painful his illness was when a family member stood up and screamed, "But this is happening to me, too! It's my illness, too!" The silence that followed was poignant. While neither denying nor minimizing the horror of those with OCD, this book focuses on the family because there are already so many good books for the OCD sufferer.[16,19,32,49,52,56,62]

When OCD strikes, it is invariably traumatic for everyone intimately connected to the sufferer. The world of trauma[34,60] is akin to looking into a fractured mirror—everything appears disjointed and disturbing. Trauma can create a life of darkness and shadows. More than the usual everyday slings and arrows of life, traumatic events are those that would be upsetting to anyone and evoke a reaction of helplessness, overwhelming fear, even terror. A strange new world unfolds, revealing astonishing layers of pain, grief, and fear.

Traumatic stress reactions appear paradoxical. On the one hand, those traumatized can't get away from the trauma. On the other hand, they can't get near it. They are overwhelmed and obsessed with it, yet they work hard to avoid it, numb themselves to it, or hide from it. Traumatized people also have physiological reactions such as exaggerated startle responses, elevated blood pressure, or insomnia.

Like the OCD sufferer, the family and loved ones may have some or all of these traumatic responses. They may feel overwhelmed and helpless, have nightmares, obsess and ruminate about the person with OCD, want to avoid the person, lose interest in life, feel detached or estranged from others, feel numb, or even have a sense of a diminished future. They may have sleep problems, be irritable or angry, have difficulty concentrating, be overly aware of others and their surroundings, be constantly frightened, or they may develop physical symptoms. These are all symptoms of "traumatic stress responses" that people can experience when they are subjected to prolonged or excessive stress. Everyone in the family can have traumatic stress reactions in response to the influence of OCD.

There is much, however, to be hopeful about. When you begin your own recovery process, it will lift your spirit, open your heart, and deepen your soul. A new world of light is beginning to shine on those who only years ago suffered in silence and shame. You don't have to wait any longer for help. There are more resources and more acceptance than ever before. Recovery is possible for you and your family. It can be viewed as a process of reclaiming who you are, discovering your strengths, and developing a rich, new relationship with yourself and your loved ones.

An Era of Emerging Hope

In winter 1985, three patients from the OCD clinic at Yale University in New Haven, Connecticut, shared the stories of their tormented, OCD-dominated lives. All three had suffered alone, in silence and in shame, hiding their symptoms for fear that they were early signs of madness. These three brave, intrepid souls realized something had to be done to reach out to the millions of other OCD sufferers who believed they also were alone. They wanted to let them know that their illness had a name and that it could be treated.[32]

From this crucible of necessity, the Obsessive-Compulsive Foundation (OC Foundation) was born. The first meeting took place in spring 1986 at the Yale clinic. Two of its founders convinced the ABC news magazine "20/20" to broadcast the first major television special to inform the public about OCD. The program aired March 19, 1987, and the floodgates opened. Soon after, psychiatrist Judith Rapoport[49] wrote a stunning bestseller, *The Boy Who Couldn't Stop Washing*. This eye-opening book took the country and the mental health professions by storm. Millions of people suddenly had a name for—and an understanding of—the illness that afflicted them or someone they loved. The first goal of the foundation and Dr. Rapoport was reached: the country was awakened to the existence of OCD. It was no longer hidden.

We are again, years later, entering another era of great excitement, great discovery, and great hope for all under the influence of OCD. Treatment centers, clinics, and hospitals with special expertise in the treatment of OCD are now located all across the United States and throughout the world. Ongoing national and international research looks into its causes and treatments. Improvements have been made in behavioral treatment through "exposure and response prevention," as well as in cognitive therapy. The Obsessive-Compulsive Information Center, in listing articles about behavior therapy through September 1997, cites 1600 references.

Although research is in its early stages, there is the suggestion that the so-called "power psychotherapies," protocols like EMDR (Eye Movement Desensitization and Reprocessing)[53,54] and TFT (Thought-Field Therapy),[7] may have some applicability in treating those with OCD as well as those impacted by its traumatic wake.

While estimates suggest that fewer than 20 percent of individuals with neurobiological disorders, such as OCD, actually receive treatment, many sufferers are finding hope and recovery through mutual or self-help groups, Obsessive-Compulsive Anonymous, professionally assisted support groups, and online computer-based support groups. Of great importance is an increased awareness of the family's needs and the needs of others close to people with OCD. Because of the groundbreaking work of pioneers like Fred Penzel, Marlene Cooper, and Barbara Livingston-VanNoppen, among others, family support and validation for both OCD sufferers and their families have become more common.[6,12,13,40,59] So, yes indeed, things are changing and possibilities are expanding!

My Path to the Work

Since we are about to go on a special journey together, it may help you to know me better. I am a licensed clinical psychologist in Santa Barbara, California. I work with individuals, groups, couples, and families. I have written or co-written other self-help books, pamphlets, and articles. In the early 1980s, I led seminars and workshops around the country for adult children of alcoholics. In 1983, I became a Founding Member of the Board of Directors of the National Association of Children of Alcoholics (NACoA), an association devoted to helping millions of children of alcoholics.

While my professional work with survivors of trauma began in the early 1980s, my personal experience started with my birth into a Holocaust family. When I was born in 1942, the Nazi persecution of millions of people was occurring. My parents lived with the uncertainty of whether their family members were alive. During my childhood years, my mother discovered that she had lost nearly her entire family.

My father, though fewer members of his family were killed, was irrevocably affected by the Holocaust also.

Ever since I was a child, I have been trying to figure out how to heal families. I even got a Ph.D. in order to better do so. I have worked with thousands of family members under the influence of alcohol, families under the influence of other addictions, families under the influence of schizophrenia, families under the influence of bipolar disorders, and now families under the influence of OCD. I am still trying to heal the family.

My path to this book was forged by my professional experience. Several encounters were especially formative. First was my work in "peer counseling," a person-helping-person approach to aiding others. From 1972 to 1978, I directed a multi-ethnic peer program at University of California Santa Barbara. Staffed by Asian, African-American, Latino, and Native American students as well as gay, lesbian, and single-mother students, the program's mission was to reach students who didn't receive traditional counseling. Through the outer workings of this diverse program, I glimpsed the inner workings of the human psyche. I learned how each part of the whole is unique, special, and vital. And I learned that the whole is greater than the sum of its parts. In terms of the family, this means that the wishes, desires, or fears of one person can't become more important than the family itself if the family is to thrive or even survive.

My second formative experience occurred in 1980, when I attended my first Employee Assistance Program (EAP) conference. EAP programs focus largely on alcoholism. Consequently, I got a good understanding of the current information in the alcohol field. I felt surprisingly comfortable and formed an immediate kinship with this work. The acceptance, love, and nurturing of this community began to fuel my own recovery as the grandchild of Holocaust survivors.

I began working with a dedicated and talented colleague, Julie D. Bowden. We began the first Adult Children of Alcoholics (ACA) psychotherapy group at the University of California, collaborated on two books, and presented workshops throughout the United States on the children of alcoholics and other children of trauma. During that period I worked with thousands of adult children from all parts of the country.

I also began to study clinical hypnosis. I saw the parallels between the trance states of hypnosis and the common issues of children of alcoholics. As a result, I viewed codependence as a deep negative trance or spell. My studies next led me to explore classical mythology, which offered a map of recovery and healing that has survived the test of time. Mythology offers the great stories throughout history with all their lessons for modern times.

As I traveled, many people told me that they did not come from alcoholic homes, but identified with the personal issues I described. I began to realize how widespread trauma is and began to focus on those who grew up in a family where any traumatic circumstance had affected the family. Those from all traumatic environments share much in common in their reactions to trauma. When upheaval strikes, everyone in the family is overwhelmed by it and attempts to avoid it. To heal, everyone must learn to move away from the upheaval's influence, move toward healing, and then move back to the family, bringing with them all that they have learned and all that they have become.

As a result, my next book was not on the traumas from alcoholic families in particular, but about traumatic experiences in general. I wrote from the perspective of trauma as a crucible for developing excellence.[26] Excellence is the process through which we turn life's wounds into gifts. While success is getting up one more time than we fall, excellence is learning to fall less and less frequently.

Thus, the groundwork for my experience with this book on OCD had been laid. My next formative experience occurred in 1991 when I met Tom, an intelligent and frightened young man with strange and confusing symptoms that I would later identify as OCD. Like many professionals, I had little experience in recognizing OCD.

Tom and I discovered his correct diagnosis at about the same time. Before diagnosing the OCD, treatment proceeded slowly. After the diagnosis, Tom's progress immediately accelerated. From my work in the recovery movement, I realized the value of inviting the families of my clients into sessions. Therefore, I suggested that Tom invite his family to a therapy session. I quickly saw that OCD was affecting his family in similar ways to any major chronic disorder,[58] especially one in which secrecy and shame affect family members. I also saw how everyone benefits when the family gets help.

From experiences with my first family living with OCD, I began to apply the valuable and hard-fought lessons from a host of disciplines to my counseling work with OCD. They encompassed lessons from recovery psychology,[5,26] from the traumatic stress literature,[33,60] from the physical healing literature,[11,39] from the psychology of excellence and personal effectiveness,[14,20,26] from studying altered states of consciousness,[17] from mythology and spirituality,[10,22] and even lessons from the new science of physics and chaos theory.[64] As my awareness in treating OCD expanded, my ability to become a healing agent for all the family members grew. With this synthesis, I have become more adept at bringing more comfort and healing to each member.

Expanding the Focus of Treatment

Understandably, the person with OCD has received most of the attention both in the doctor's office and in the public's eye. The majority of what has been written about this disorder centers around those with OCD and their compulsions, obsessions, and compulsive rituals. Meanwhile, the family has often had to adapt and organize itself around the person with the illness, receiving little if any validation, support, or direct help itself. When help has been available to the family, it has often been presented as advice on how to help and support the person with OCD.

Because OCD is a stress-sensitive disorder, the more stress that is present, the more the person with OCD suffers. As a result, there tends to be pressure on loved ones to act in certain ways around those with OCD in order to help them manage their symptoms or minimize their stress. The loved ones begin to focus more and more on the person with OCD and begin to lose sight of their own wants and needs, and even lose sight of themselves.[6,13,25,26,40,59]

You, the family and other loved ones, have often been discounted, brushed to the side, and overlooked. Your fears, your problems, your disappointments, your hopes, your aspirations, and your own growth have come second to those with OCD. Even though you are the "healthy one," loving someone with OCD has changed your life. Watching the people you love gripped by seemingly strange forces beyond their control is a difficult experience. And changing your own priorities, routines, ideas, and beliefs to accommodate OCD results in personal losses. These losses may trigger strong feelings of grief in you also.

Overview of This Book

A momentum occurs in every healing process. It always begins with surviving the injury or circumstance. Early in the process of dealing with OCD, both the person with OCD and the family with OCD are drowning in a conspiracy of denial and ignorance. Failure to recognize the OCD and to acknowledge its effects on the person as well as the family creates an atmosphere of fear, confusion, grief, and exhaustion.

When a diagnosis is made, both the person with OCD and the family under its influence begin to move into a stage of discovery and emerging awareness. Ignorance is not bliss. We cannot change those things of which we are not aware. In the next stage of healing and recovery, both the person with OCD and the family can move beyond the diagnosis and begin to understand the ongoing issues in which they get stuck.

Healing occurs as core issues become transformed into life-enhancing habits. Major shifts in thoughts, feelings, and behaviors unfold and lead to an increasing sense of personal integration. Movement through these stages can lead both the person with OCD and the family to embrace the wounding, put it into perspective, and in the last stage find the gift it can reveal.

This progression through stages of recovery and healing, from moving into awareness, moving away from the trauma, moving toward healing, and returning with the gift, is occurring in more and more families throughout the country. Healing is an attainable goal for all persons under the influence of OCD.

This book is divided into eight chapters that break down the process described above. Together, we will review the overall healing and recovery process that the family, offspring, and other loved ones of the person with OCD may move through. More specifically, the book is organized as follows:

- In Chapter One, you learn about the devastating illness of OCD and its impact on the person as well as the family and other loved ones.

- In Chapter Two, you meet the family with OCD and learn what happens to them.

- In Chapter Three, you become aware of the physical, emotional, and spiritual impact of OCD on the family and other loved ones.

- In Chapter Four, you learn what problems or core issues can develop in reaction to, and as a result of, living with someone who has OCD.

- In Chapter Five, you learn how to move beyond your problems, to transform them, and to heal yourself.

- In Chapter Six, you learn to move toward your own healing, get your life back, accept the illness, and gain a growing sense of confidence.

- In Chapter Seven, you move back to the family with all of the knowledge and strength you have acquired.

- In Chapter Eight, you learn a variety of practical and concrete strategies for dealing with everyday concerns.

The book closes with an inspiring note from Robin, an OCD sufferer, who shares her insights.

Also included are two appendices that contain extensive resources to help you learn more about OCD and its impact upon the family.

Appendix A contains information about where to get further help.

Appendix B is a list of other books to read about OCD and family healing.

Reading This Book

Based on the many questions I am asked in my clinical practice, I have chosen to present this information in a question-and-answer format. You may already know much of what is discussed on one level, yet you may not understand how much you really know on another. My task is to help you recognize what you know, organize it in a useful manner, validate what you are feeling, and make all of this knowledge more accessible to you. Even so, the answers are often complicated, elusive, and partial. It is impossible to capture the diversity or complexity of families through words alone.

In addition, I can't possibly answer all of your questions and may have left out questions that are very important to you. Continue to search for answers to those questions and, more importantly, learn to trust your own experience. I apologize ahead of time for any incompleteness. There is still so much to learn about families under the influence of OCD. The field is just climbing out of its adolescence. I am reminded of one of my favorite scenes in the original "Star Trek" television series. Brave Captain Kirk and his dedicated doctor, "Bones," were on a planet in a faraway galaxy. "Bones" turned to Captain Kirk and said, "Can you believe that these people still cut into people to heal them?" I hope that in five or ten years, when we look back on our present treatment of OCD and its effects on family members, we will be similarly astounded.

Reading this book may very well arouse strong feelings. OCD is still a hidden disorder and shrouded in secrecy. The disorder is still enveloped by shame. That's why the majority of people with OCD and their families get little or no help. Even when they do reach out for assistance, they're apt to get help from someone who has little understanding of the unique situation in which they are embroiled. When this happens, a personal tragedy can become a disaster for everyone.

At times, this book may be difficult for you to read. It may also be difficult for those with OCD who, more often than not, are painfully aware of the hurt and distress they have caused loved ones. Like others with chronic ailments,[58,61] the emotional difficulties of those with OCD are compounded when they're aware that their behavior touches off feelings of anger and revulsion in others instead of the love and compassion they need. Many people with OCD report being repulsed themselves by their own seemingly uncontrollable and bizarre behavior.

You may notice your experiences do not match everything described here. Use this book as a place to begin. Take what is helpful and simply leave the rest. Remember, it is up to you to decide what kinds of changes, if any, you want to make in your life and how this book can best serve your needs.

The healing effect of the material works best when read in sequence. Feel free to read some, put the book down and take a walk, talk to a friend, or do anything that feeds and nourishes you. It is important to develop support to help you as you work through your feelings and start the process of your change. Be gentle with yourself as you digest your new understanding of OCD's impact on you and your family.

Reading this book is not unlike the good news/bad news joke about early- and late-stage recovery. The good news comes in early-stage recovery when we learn that "It's not our fault." The bad news in late recovery is, "Everything is our responsibility." This doesn't mean we are to blame for anything. It just means being responsible for our life is a much more empowering place to stand. While the good news about this book is that there is recovery, the bad news is that we have to work hard for it. If this book is to help you, it will require your rigorous integrity and commitment to your healing. It will require no less than everything you have.

The serious reader will come to understand that there are no shortcuts. Our most important internal resources may be what noted psychiatrist M. Scott Peck,[47] in *The Road Less Traveled,* calls discipline: delaying gratification, accepting responsibility, and dedicating ourselves to the truth. Perhaps the most important external resource is the companionship of others who are traveling along the same path. Little can replace the validation, acceptance, support, and love of those who understand. We need what the Swiss psychiatrist Alice Miller calls "enlightened witnesses" to endure the journey. We need to both witness others' journeys and be witnessed ourselves. When the journey evokes difficult feelings, others provide the mirroring that lets us know we are headed in the right direction.

The feelings evoked by this book may require similar mirroring. They may vary from light to dark, from hope to despair, from skepticism to belief. All of these feelings are natural and normal, and your specific feelings probably indicate your own special needs. They may provide the awareness most helpful at this stage of your recovery.

There are good reasons for all the different feelings and reactions you may have. The message of this book is to talk, to trust, to feel, to question, to think, and to be, all of which run counter to the rules in a family experiencing trauma.[27] Breaking the rules and following the suggestions in this book are enough to make anyone feel frightened and guilty. Even the experienced traveler is not immune to fear and doubt.

Many of you may feel validated as you read this book because it will correspond to your own experiences. Many will experience relief. At the same time, you may experience the shock of recognition as some story, some example, touches you personally and deeply. Expect to experience a wide variety of emotions as you progress through the material.

Finally, a word should be said about references in this book. Many readers will not want to be distracted by the citing of references. Some readers, however, might be interested in delving further into a particular topic and want its reference cited. To accommodate both, I have placed the appropriate references as a superscript so they will be unobtrusive to the reader.

—⚏—

CHAPTER 1

Origins and Beginnings— The Web of OCD

—ᙢ—

Who Are You?

If you have picked up this book, it is likely that you are dealing with someone who can act quite strangely, even bizarrely, at times. It could be a friend, someone with whom you work, your car mechanic, or the person down the street. But, it can also be a family member or other loved one, like your child, spouse, parent, sibling, aunt, or uncle.

You might be a pioneer, the first in your family or group to notice that something is really wrong. You may be a seasoned veteran who has been dealing with a family member with OCD for a long time. You might even be someone impacted by other serious, chronic mental disorders like schizophrenia, bipolar disorder, major depression, or a physical disease like lupus or chronic fatigue.

Regardless, you are a person most likely committed to extending your own knowledge and personal effectiveness, a person willing to take the time and attention needed to heal from what can be a devastating emotional, mental, physical, and spiritual problem: being caught in the web of OCD or another chronic condition.

What Is OCD?

Each of us worries occasionally. But suppose your brain's ability to stop worrying goes haywire? You would get no rest from the everyday worries we all have. And, what if you could never stop worrying? Obviously, you would worry and worry and engage in whatever behaviors that seemed to reduce the worry. You would have OCD.

OCD is classified in the 4th edition of the *Diagnostic and Statistical Manual of Mental Disorders* (called *DSM-IV* by professional mental health practitioners) as an anxiety disorder. This means that it is one of a group of disorders that have fear and avoidance as their primary symptoms. Other anxiety disorders include panic disorder, agoraphobia, social phobia, generalized anxiety disorder, and post-traumatic stress disorder.

OCD affects males and females equally, and those with it are besieged by irrational fears that don't easily go away. They often have elaborate strategies to try and decrease these fears. Paradoxically, these elaborate strategies or compulsive behaviors actually result in more, not less, anxiety. While these thoughts and behaviors may seem "crazy," both to the person with OCD and to the people observing the behavior, a person with OCD is not "crazy." They are having a normal reaction to fear gone haywire.

Following heredity more than socioeconomic status, OCD strikes the poor and the rich alike, the educated and the uneducated. Although it typically appears in childhood or early adulthood, it can strike at any age.[34] Many believe the famous billionaire Howard Hughes died alone and estranged because of this debilitating and potentially life-threatening illness. Other major figures in history have been identified as probably suffering from OCD, including religious leader Martin Luther, author John Bunyan *(The Pilgrim's Progress),* and poet and statesman Samuel Johnson.

Several sports figures have been open about their OCD. Hockey goalie Clint Malarchuk speaks candidly about how his OCD drove him to retrace his car routes endlessly to make sure he hadn't run over anyone. Florida Marlins baseball player Jim Eisenreich and Denver Nuggets basketball player Mahmoud Abdul-Rauf (formerly Chris Jackson) have been open about their Tourette's disorder, a related illness featuring tics, grunts, and the uttering of strings of obscenities.

Marc Summers, host of the children's game show "Double Dare," shared his experiences with OCD on "Oprah" and "Dateline." He described his terror when he would come home and feel compelled to clean for hours, even after the house was thoroughly clean. He also described his wife awakening in the middle of the night to find him cleaning and straightening all of the "fringe" on the carpets in the house, which he had been doing secretly for years.

What Are Obsessions?

The term obsession comes from the Latin *obsidere,* to besiege. Obsessions are recurrent, persistent, intrusive thoughts, images, ideas, or impulses that seem to arise out of nowhere. They can render their victims powerless, as the person may come to believe that they have little or no control over them. These disturbing and tenacious thoughts have been described as "hiccups of the brain" by psychiatrist Judith Rapoport[49] or as a sensation that the brain is "stuck in gear" by psychiatrist Jeffrey Schwartz.[52]

The most common obsessions are repeated thoughts about contamination, such as fear of germs, repeated doubts (ruminating whether one has performed some act like checking appliances, doors, or windows), a need to have things in a particular order (severe discomfort when objects are asymmetrical or disordered), aggressive or horrific impulses (hurting a child or shouting blasphemies in church or synagogue), or abhorrent sexual imagery (recurrent pornographic images).[21] People with OCD seem unable to "shake the idea" or "let go" of the obsessive thought or idea. They usually doubt their own senses and are unable to trust themselves.

These intrusive and persistent obsessive thoughts and images vary from person to person, as well as from time to time, but they usually revolve around the potential of harm to oneself or others.

What Are Compulsions?

Compulsions are repeated behaviors or mental acts performed in order to decrease the fear and anxiety generated by obsessive thoughts or images.[1] These ritualized behaviors are performed to manage the fear generated by the frightening and obsessive thoughts. Compulsive behaviors, however, create only an illusion of control because the rituals don't achieve the desired relief. The compulsions may initially lessen the anxiety and have a calming effect, but over time this positive effect lessens and persons with OCD find that they must alter and/or increase the rituals in order to obtain relief.

Common compulsions involve cleaning and washing, checking, hoarding, requesting or demanding assurances, repeated actions, counting, and ordering. These seemingly irrational behaviors can include hand washing to the point of damage to the skin, washing clothes and surroundings over and over again, or checking doors and appliances to make sure they're secured or turned off.[56] These activities can consume so much time and energy that people are literally unable to leave their homes. They may have difficulty getting to work, having relationships, even getting to bed at a reasonable time because the compulsions demand so much of their time.

What Are Other Symptoms Associated With OCD?

Depression and anxiety are two common symptoms that often accompany OCD.[32] In fact, one researcher estimates that 90 percent of OCD sufferers experience a major depression at some point in their illness. Dr. Lewis Baxter, OCD researcher at the University of California Los Angeles and the University of Alabama, states that two-thirds of OCD patients will suffer depression. Severe depression can lead to suicidal thoughts and actions.

The addition of anxiety problems is another associated factor. Many persons with OCD suffer from a high degree of anxiety that includes panic attacks and various types of phobias. Some people become homebound, afraid to leave the relative safety of their homes. The social functioning and skills of those with OCD are often poor.

Several other forms of behavior may be related to OCD. They are often called "Obsessive-Compulsive Spectrum Disorders"[62] and include the following: hair pulling (trichotillomania), preoccupation with an imagined body defect (body dysmorphic disorder), severe nail biting, and/or the fear of serious illness (hypochondriasis). Some eating disorders may be incorrectly diagnosed when the symptoms are really OCD fears of contamination. Other diagnostic categories that overlap with OCD are certain neurological disorders such as Tourette's syndrome, Huntington's chorea, torticollis, autism, and Asperger's syndrome. In addition, disorders with prominent impulsive and aggressive features like pathological gambling, kleptomania, compulsive buying or spending, and certain compulsive self-mutilation or self-injurious syndromes may be related.

Are There Different Types of OCD?

There are many different types of OCD. The most typical kinds of obsessions and compulsions are washing and cleaning, checking, counting and repeating, ordering, hoarding, ritualistic thinking, strange movements, and worrying or pure obsessing.

Some people with OCD are so afraid of contamination from germs that they spend hours daily washing and sterilizing themselves and may insist that the people they live with do the same. They may feel fearful about allowing others to enter their homes; they may refuse to leave their homes; or they may even be unable to touch those they love for fear of contamination. These people are often referred to as "washers" and "cleaners."

"Checkers," the second most common group of persons with OCD, are driven by a need to prevent a disaster they fear may happen as a result of their careless actions. They may obsessively worry that they have hit someone with their car and will stop in terror and retrace their route many times. They check their cars for dents and scratches and the pavement for any signs of blood. Still, they doubt their own senses and must return to check again and again.

Fearing they have left a stove burner on or some other appliance running that will set the house on fire and hurt someone, "checkers" will return again and again, sometimes dozens of times a day, to check and make sure they have turned off all the appliances, locked the doors, or turned off the faucets and light switches. They fear that, as a result of their negligence, the house will burn down, a burglar will enter and rob and hurt their family, or the house will flood, drowning everyone. Those plagued with checking compulsions don't trust themselves and must try to reassure themselves over and over again—or sometimes be reassured by others—that all has been done correctly so that no disasters will occur.

Some persons with OCD have such unpleasant sexual and/or religious thoughts that they act out elaborate and exhausting rituals to compensate for these frightening or "sinful" thoughts and ideas. "Repeaters," when viewed in a religious context, are said to be suffering from scrupulosity. Priests, ministers, and rabbis have noted over the centuries that some people in their churches indulged in excessive prayer, unreasonable doubting, and extreme fastidiousness. Other activities "repeaters" do to ward off catastrophe include repeating an action until it feels just "right" or repeating a physical or mental ritual until the "bad" thought goes away. Trying to prevent yourself from having a thought is a losing battle, and the type and frequency of the compensating compulsions only increases over time. For example, try not to think of pink elephants.

Arranging possessions in a precise, exact manner is another way persons with OCD may attempt to exert control and to drive away their fears. "Orderers" are driven by a need to be sure things are arranged in a certain way. This may include closets, contents of drawers, pictures, and/or furniture. Coming back in a room and discovering that something has been moved, however slightly, can cause great distress and even anger in individuals who have this type of OCD.

Hoarding is still another common form of OCD. "Hoarders" hang on to items out of fear that they may part with something valuable that they might need someday. People with this variation of OCD and their families are sometimes forced to live in progressively smaller spaces as their possessions fill up their house or apartment. When taken to the extreme, "hoarders" can force other family members to move to the basement or even outside. Occasionally they are visited by the health department or evicted from their apartment.

Other less common forms of OCD may include mental ritualizers or "pure obsessionals." These sufferers try to allay their distress by using internal arguments or performing specific and precise mental routines. While the obsessions and compulsions of OCD vary, the common threads are thoughts and images of harm, and actions designed to reduce the fear.

Are OCD and Obsessive-Compulsive Personality Disorder Similar or the Same?

OCD is very different from Obsessive-Compulsive Personality Disorder. Those who have a personality disorder don't have true compulsions or obsessions. Instead, they have a pervasive pattern of pre-occupation with orderliness, perfectionism, and control at the expense of flexibility, openness, and efficiency. They are unaware of how annoyed others become when they have to deal with their excessively rigid and stubborn behaviors. Furthermore, unlike OCD, which can occur at any point in life, the person with an Obsessive-Compulsive Personality Disorder must have formed this disorder by early adulthood.

In moderation, obsessive-compulsive personality traits may be useful, especially in situations or tasks that require attention to detail and thoroughness. For instance, I want the editor of this book to have obsessive-compulsive traits, and you would want your dentist to have them as well. Only when these traits result in maladaptiveness and cause significant impairment or subjective distress do they constitute Obsessive-Compulsive Personality Disorder.

What Causes OCD? Is It a Biological Disease?
Is It Genetic? Is It Just in the Person's Mind?

In truth, no one really knows why some people develop the disorder. At this point, the exact cause or causes of OCD are unknown. There seem, however, to be several contributing factors, including disturbances in brain function, genetics, behavioral factors, familial patterns, trauma, and stress. Most experts[36] believe OCD is a biochemical disorder with a genetic predisposition and that both biological and psychological causes exist.

OCD researchers have identified a specific brain structure that is implicated. Apparently, any damage to this primary brain structure, the caudate nucleus, whether from bad genes, head trauma, or even from the body's own immune system, can result in OCD. In fact, it has been known to develop in children as a result of a strep throat infection. The same antibody that attacks strep can also attack the caudate nucleus, causing a child to develop OCD. Treatment with blood plasma and antibiotics makes these symptoms decline noticeably. There is clear evidence that certain centers in the brain do not function normally in people with OCD. Brain imaging technology (PET scans are one brain imaging technique) gives us clues as to the regions of the brain that aren't working properly. Certain brain messengers, or neurotransmitters (serotonin in particular), do not seem to be functioning properly in persons with OCD. The success of certain medications is probably related to their normalizing effects on brain neurotransmitter functioning, particularly serotonin levels.

With regard to genetics, there seems to be a strong familial pattern to OCD occurrence.[34] Studies at the National Institute of Mental Health in Bethesda, Maryland, show that one in four people with OCD have had a close family member with OCD. Some families have at least four successive generations with clear cases of Obsessive-Compulsive Disorder. Other experts report a familial prevalence of 20 to 30 percent. Studies of identical and fraternal twins also provide some evidence that there is an inherited component in Obsessive-Compulsive Disorder. It is difficult to estimate the occurrence of OCD, since sufferers have tended to keep their disorder a secret. Also, there may be elements of OCD which are "learned" behaviors. Regardless, there does seem to be a definite familial connection.

There is also evidence that overall family functioning and stress levels may be important in the development and expression of OCD. While these factors do not "cause" OCD, family dysfunction and increased stress can be contributing factors in the development of OCD in predisposed persons. While we do know that OCD is not caused by personality structure or unconscious wishes, drives, or conflicts, these can also exacerbate symptoms.

It is important to remember that biology does not determine destiny. Just because there are occurrences of OCD in your family does not mean you will ever get OCD. Furthermore, if you or loved one develops OCD symptoms, this does not mean that you or your loved one will be unable to overcome them.

Is It Your Fault?

It is clear that no one "causes" OCD in another, yet it's natural to feel responsible. It is a strategy designed by your unconscious or subconscious mind to give you some feeling of control. "If I am to blame, then I can control it." But we aren't responsible for what we can't control. It is helpful to remember the four C's of Al-Anon, the 12-Step program for the family and loved ones of alcoholics: you did not cause it, you cannot control it, you cannot cure it, but you can cope with it. By learning to cope with OCD, you can impact its course and outcome. You can also respond to OCD in ways that will help both the person with OCD and you and other family members as well.

How Many People Have OCD?

OCD was once thought to be rare. We now know that this is not true.[50] The Obsessive-Compulsive Foundation (OC Foundation) estimates that up to 3 percent of the U.S. population (about five or six million people) may suffer from OCD at some point in their lives. Other

OCD experts estimate that as many as seven-and-a-half to eight million people have the disorder, which would place it as the fourth most common of all mental disorders, behind phobias, depression, and alcoholism.[62] It is nearly as common as asthma and diabetes.

In addition to the pain and misery that this poorly understood affliction causes individuals and their family members, it is a financially draining illness also. In the *Wall Street Journal* in 1995, one mental health authority asserted that OCD costs the U.S. economy more than eight billion dollars a year, a conservative estimate because this figure doesn't include lost income. It is clear that OCD is a common—and costly—mental health disorder that affects millions.

What Happens Over Time to the Person With OCD?

OCD is an illness that waxes and wanes over time. This means it is like riding a roller coaster without ever stopping. The sufferer may be relatively symptom-free for days or weeks, even months, when suddenly the disease strikes again. Symptoms often come from out of nowhere, and the sufferer feels as though he or she has been blindsided. There is often an initial sense of guilt when you, a family member, worry that you could have prevented the episode, "if only you had been more patient or hadn't upset the person with OCD." There is, however, really nothing you could have done to prevent it.

Some sufferers seem to outgrow OCD while others move into a progressively debilitating chronic disorder with the symptoms increasing in severity. The *DSM-IV* states that "about 15 percent show progressive deterioration in occupational and social functioning. Conversely, about 5 percent have an episodic course with minimal or no symptoms between episodes."

For most OCD sufferers, compulsions tend to become entrenched and behaviors get cemented over time. As the thoughts become more frequent and intrusive, compulsive rituals increase, and people feel further imprisoned by their fears and behaviors. And, as the rituals lose their power to decrease the anxiety, the person with OCD is caught in a terrifying, exhausting, and debilitating cycle of obsession and compulsion.

Early diagnosis and treatment can therefore have a profound effect on the course of OCD and can result in the person leading a more normal life.

How Will You Know If Your Loved One Has OCD and If It Is Severe Enough to Warrant Professional Attention?

We all have habits and superstitions. Some people seem by nature to be concerned with cleanliness and order in their lives. Others perform minor rituals that are comforting to them, and we all "check" to some degree. Some of these personality traits and behaviors might look like OCD, but they are not. While these "habits" may cause inconvenience and annoyance for the person who has them and for his or her family, they are not in the form of unwanted and intrusive thoughts and compulsive behaviors that they cannot control. These patterns of behavior, while sometimes chronic, are more a part of a person's personality and way of behaving than something that seems to come upon them from outside themselves.

In deciding if the OCD warrants professional help, you can look at how it impacts the life of the person with OCD and how it impacts your life. Does OCD affect the person's normal functioning? Can the person with OCD stop his behaviors? How long does the person spend performing rituals or compulsions? How debilitating are they? Can the person work (assuming the person is old enough)? And are the symptoms putting stress on the person and the family? It would be helpful to look at the amount and frequency of the symptoms, and the impact of OCD on the person's interpersonal relationships, play, work, and family life. If this impact is substantial, it is time to seek help. Both you and the person with OCD may need it. It may also be important to determine how much denial and minimization are occurring about the effects of the OCD on everyone.

How Is OCD Treated?

Effective treatment for OCD is available. Current research in the United States indicates that OCD does not respond to "talk therapies," such as insight-oriented psychotherapy, which explore the underlying causes and dynamics behind symptoms. While traditional psychotherapy is often not useful in reducing the OCD symptoms, it may be useful in helping people with OCD cope more effectively with the illness, their relationships, and their lives. Conventional wisdom among OCD specialists is that OCD is not cured. Instead, it is treated by managing symptoms, so that the person can lead an essentially normal life.

Today's treatment is usually a combination of drug therapy and behavior therapy. Cognitive therapy is also used and, rarely, electroconvulsive therapy, and very rarely psychosurgery.[32] Drug therapy has been helpful for many. In the brain, nerves send messages through substances called neurotransmitters. Serotonin, one of these brain messengers, appears to be involved in OCD. Thus, the most successfully used drugs in the treatment of OCD are those that affect the serotonin activity in the brain. The most common of these drugs are clomipramine (Anafranil), fluoxetine (Prozac), fluvoxamine (Luvox), paroxetine (Paxil), and sertraline (Zoloft). All of these drugs can have side effects and typically take eight to twelve weeks to be effective in reducing the obsessive thoughts and compulsive behaviors of OCD. Often, the medications provide enough reduction in anxiety to allow the patient to progress with other forms of therapy.

Behavior therapy[19] in the form of "exposure and response prevention," is a frequently used technique. The person with OCD is encouraged to gradually expose himself to the fearful situations or behaviors that would usually cause obsessive thoughts and compulsive urges; and then to learn to resist these compulsions. For example, those who endlessly check the locks on their doors would be encouraged to try to lock them once for a pre-determined length of time and then to cope with the feeling of panic that follows. These urges will lessen with time as the compulsions are resisted. But never underestimate how difficult it is for OCD sufferers to begin the initial efforts to prevent the compulsive response.

Cognitive therapy works to help patients learn new ways of thinking about and responding to the thoughts and urges that come with OCD. Those with OCD learn to recognize certain thoughts as coming from their illness or "stuck brain" and to replace those thoughts with more positive ones. They also practice challenging the seeming absolute truth of these beliefs. One recognized expert in the treatment of OCD encourages his patients when they think these thoughts to tell themselves, "It's not me, it's my OCD!"[52] Remember also that OCD is not the sum total of who the person is anymore than someone with cancer is just his or her cancer.

Many OCD treatment professionals find a combination of proper medication and behavioral therapy to be of great help. Brain scans shows that either method, or both in combination, alter brain chemistry in measurable ways. These treatments seem to help the brain to be less "stuck" in repetitive thought patterns. Medication and behavior therapy in combination work well for more than 70 to 80 percent of OCD patients.

As with many illnesses, and especially OCD, early diagnosis and treatment maximize the recovery. As research continues, newer drugs and therapy techniques will evolve. You and your loved one must be patient and persistent in seeking treatment. Stay informed and don't give up. There is help for both the person with OCD and the family (See Appendices A and B).

Is There a National Organization for People With OCD?

Yes! For information, education, support, and current research, contact the OC Foundation (See Appendix A), a worldwide organization, whose primary goal is to let OCD sufferers know they are not alone, that they are not crazy, and that their OCD is not the result of personal weakness or a traumatic childhood. The foundation is dedicated to early intervention, to controlling and finding cures for OCD, and to improving the welfare of people with this disorder. The foundation distributes the most up-to-date information available on OCD by providing relevant publications and audio and videotapes. The OC Foundation Newsletter, published six times a year, keeps those with OCD and their family members informed of the latest advances in the field. Dissemination of information to medical, educational, and

governmental professionals, and lobbying efforts to eliminate discrimi-
nation are additional priorities. This organization also seeks to advance
knowledge of OCD through supporting formal research. The foundation offers lists of self-help support groups and even puts individual
sufferers in contact with other members who have OCD.

What Resources, Apart From Professional Treatment, Are Available to Those With OCD?

Fortunately, there are many resources available and their numbers
are increasing. Appendix A lists many of them. There is no longer *any*
reason for *any* sufferer of OCD or *any* family member under its influence to suffer alone, without help and comfort!

One resource that emphasizes a spiritual approach to healing is
Obsessive-Compulsive Anonymous (OCA).[45] OCA offers help directly
to the person with OCD and indirectly to the loved ones. Established
in January 1988, OCA is a self-help, 12-Step program based on the
principles of Alcoholics Anonymous (commonly known as AA), which
has helped countless alcoholics throughout the world.

The foreword to *Obsessive-Compulsive Anonymous,* the "Big
Book" of OCA, states: OCA "is a fellowship of people who share their
experience, strength, and hope with each other that they may solve
their common problem and help others to recover from Obsessive-
Compulsive Disorder (OCD). The only requirement for membership
is a desire to recover from OCD. There are no dues or fees; we are
self-supporting through our own contributions. OCA is not allied with
any sect, denomination, politics, organization, or institution; it does
not wish to engage in any controversy, neither endorses nor opposes
any causes. Our primary purpose is to recover from OCD and to help
others." OCA does not provide psychological or counseling services,
nor does it make referrals to qualified professionals.

Recovery through OCA is defined as follows: "...relief obtained
from our obsessions and compulsions as a result of working the 12-
Step program. Total abstinence from OCD is *not* our focus—instead
we focus on our daily application of the program and its incorporation

into our lives. This emphasis will result in a reduction of OCD symptoms and a state of well-being."

Another increasingly available resource for families under the influence of OCD is a family-helping approach called the Journey of Hope (JOH). Originally geared for families under the influence of schizophrenia, bipolar disorders, and the major depressions, JOH offers more and more help to families under the influence of OCD. I will describe this organization in greater detail in a later chapter.

Should Anyone Else Be Treated?

Only rarely does OCD not affect the family. It can, and often does, become a family illness. As early as 1989, OCD specialist Barbara VanNoppen[40] noted, "Family members usually feel distraught, bewildered, overwhelmed, and frustrated." She went on to write, "Perhaps in no other psychiatric disorder is the family so inexorably brought into the patient's illness than OCD." Still later in 1993, she wrote, "Family conflict inevitably results." Marital discord, separation, divorce, alcohol abuse, and poor school performance are common results of the stress that OCD puts on both the patient and family members.[59] It is not unusual for family members to blame themselves for their child's or spouse's illness. Advice from friends and relatives may further reinforce the family's sense of shame and guilt.

Like co-alcoholism or codependence, there is a parallel disorder that strikes those closely related to and affected by the person with OCD. It unfolds as family members struggle to adapt and to protect the family, and thereby inadvertently "enable" the person with OCD. Because the family atmosphere is typically crisis oriented, often explosive, and at times abusive, the spouses, the children, the parents, the brothers, the sisters, the grandparents, even the friends, can all develop emotional, mental, physical, and spiritual problems.

OCD is an illness of denial, secrecy, and shame. Like sufferers of OCD, "para-OCDs" (a term I use for family members whose lives are impacted by a person with OCD) often endure their disorder alone and isolated. Frequently, its sufferers are not seen as having a problem. Consequently, its millions of sufferers are ignored and minimized by those in the health care fields. Without effective intervention and outreach to the family, damaging effects can range from mild to incapacitating. Affected family members need to know that they are neither sick nor neurotic. They are simply traumatized. The family must be taught to see OCD as an illness that can affect everyone. Only after they are recognized and helped can children, parents, siblings, and spouses lovingly and effectively give appropriate support to the person with OCD.

CHAPTER 2

Under the Influence— Drowning in the Sea of Chaos

—⟋⟋⟋—

What Is Home Like in a Family Under the Influence of OCD?

In general, a troubled family is easy to spot. People are uncomfortable, their faces look strained and tense, their voices are loud and aggressive, or meek and timid, and there is little evidence of joy, affection, and nurturance. Unspoken rules guide what is permissible and what is not. Isolation and disconnection from family members and loved ones exists inside and outside the immediate family. Communication is limited and often indirect.

The atmosphere or emotional tone in a family under the influence of OCD varies, depending on the stage of awareness and healing in which the family finds itself. Before recognizing the need for recovery, often both the person with OCD and the family with OCD live in ignorance and denial. Failure to recognize OCD and to acknowledge its effects creates the most damaging family environment. Yet, this may be one of the most common emotional atmospheres in homes where OCD resides.

Such a home or "family culture" can be characterized by *chronic shock, chronic loss, chronic grief,* and *chronic exhaustion.* Although the person with OCD does not consciously intend to, he or she can dominate the family through stubbornness, intimidation, embarrassment, and fear. Everything and everyone can revolve around the person with OCD. All decisions, from minor ones like what and where to eat, to major issues like rearing children or purchasing a house, can become funneled through the illness.

As a result, family members fear doing anything that might set off the person with OCD. Because obsessions and compulsions are illogical and variable, some days are worse than others. You may know some of the things that set off OCD, but since it is so unpredictable you can never be sure. Therefore, stress and fear can be staples in the home. The atmosphere can be crisis oriented, with everyone waiting for and reacting to the next crisis. Family members are afraid to relax because they are never sure of what may happen. They can feel besieged and harassed by the illness. When this happens, they are in a state of *chronic shock.*

OCD invariably involves some sort of loss, whether it is a loss of a complete relationship with the person with OCD, a loss of a social life, a loss of personal time and energy due to the time spent dealing with OCD, a loss of leisure, a financial loss, a loss of privacy, a loss of control, or a loss of hope. The family culture is saturated with *chronic loss.* One of the consequences is a constant feeling of being alone.

When these losses aren't acknowledged, those under the influence can experience *chronic grief* as well. The frustration and helplessness that follow can create an atmosphere of guilt and subsequently resentment and anger, all formidable burdens on any family. To make matters worse, the secrecy can create an atmosphere of shame.

Because OCD can rear its head at any time, there is a state of constant expectation that if something bad can happen, it will. The result, of course, is *chronic exhaustion.*

Given this atmosphere of ongoing *stress, loss, grief,* and *exhaustion* permeating the family, it is easy to understand why family members under the influence of OCD can feel any or all of the following: helpless, confused, frightened, angry, manipulated, controlled, terrified, hesitant, tentative, cautious, indecisive, guilty, humiliated, sad, bad, crazy, protective, embarrassed, ashamed, distant, and worried. And the result of all these powerful and uncomfortable feelings can be a sense of drowning in emotion.

Further, the heaviness of the atmosphere can be compounded by the secondary effects of other concurrent disorders such as substance abuse and depression as well as life's problems such as separation, divorce, and desertion.

How Do Family Members Adjust to This Environment?

Without a clear understanding of what's going on or how to help, everyone is trying to cope on their own. Like all families, families under the influence of OCD often adjust by creating their own rules and roles to adapt to the chaos. These rules and roles create some sense of control over the unpredictability that is often characteristic of a family under the influence of OCD.

When the family lives by rules and roles designed to avoid confronting the effects of OCD, they adjust to the OCD. For example, family members may engage in checking or other enabling behaviors. Adjustment in this sense is illusionary, because what is actually occurring is an unhealthy accommodation to the strange and bizarre behaviors of the person with OCD. This type of "adjustment" can create isolation among family members who no longer communicate or experience intimacy with each other. Furthermore, this type of adjustment can actually perpetuate OCD, break the family apart, or cause problems in family members. What was originally designed to be a positive, helpful response to an acute crisis becomes a negative, unhealthy reaction to a chronic situation.

The adjustment to this unpredictable environment, however, doesn't have to be damaging if there is help in managing the repercussions OCD can create. By changing or transforming the family, the suffering can end and members can adjust in a positive way. They learn to move from "caretakers" to "caregivers." They stop reacting to the OCD and start responding to the situation.

What Rules Guide a Family With OCD?

Every family has rules.[28] Rules are the unspoken and spoken guidelines that instill attitudes, expectations, and goals for a family; they determine who has the power and authority; and they dictate how, what, when, where, and in what ways members communicate. Rules either detract from the family functioning or enhance it. Before recovery, rules tend to be dysfunctional and decrease the well-being of all family members. As the family becomes healthier, revised rules become more functional guidelines and contribute to stability, safety, and security.

Dysfunctional rules tend to be rigid, discouraging change and making little or no room for differences in people or events. Dysfunctional rules are unrealistic, impossible to keep, and encourage dishonesty, deception, and manipulation. They also limit communication and create isolation and disconnection. "Never raise your voice," "Don't trust other people," or "Never share your feelings" are examples of dysfunctional rules that weaken the family.

Prior to the recovery of a family under the influence of OCD, the number one, and often implicit rule, is that the OCD is the most important circumstance in the family. That's why so many decisions become organized around the OCD. A second rule is that everyone in the family must be an "enabler." This means everyone must cover up, take over the responsibilities, and accept the "rules" of the OCD. No one may say what he means or mean what he says, and no one can talk about what is going on—either to a family member or to someone outside. Families under the influence of OCD become very invested in keeping things the same: the status quo must be maintained at all costs. In other words, a major rule is "Don't rock the boat."

In an effort to create some sense of safety, you may have made these kinds of decisions: "If I don't talk, nobody will know how I feel and I won't get hurt. If I don't ask, I can't get rejected. If I'm invisible, I'll be okay. If I'm careful, no one will get upset. If I stop feeling, I won't have any pain." You may have learned to tiptoe, "walking on eggshells," around the person with OCD. You may have learned that it isn't safe to express your own feelings in such an atmosphere and that your own growth and needs may have become a low priority.

In addition to these general rules, there may be specific rules that apply to particular families. For example, in some families under the influence of OCD, there may be little room to walk into a room or even into the house because there is so much clutter, while in other families you must shower or hose yourself off before entering the house or touching anything. These specific rules are overt or readily evident. There are covert or hidden rules, however, that might include, "Don't challenge," "Don't say the obvious," and especially, "Don't do anything that might trigger the OCD." All of these dysfunctional rules are rigid and unhealthy. They restrict choice and growth and may prevent you from exploring alternative behaviors. In addition, they may hinder the recovery of the person with OCD.

Functional rules, on the other hand, foster direct communication and lead the way toward accountability and responsibility instead of blame and denial, two aspects that drive dysfunction. "Respect others' rights," "Honor privacy," or "Pick up after yourself" are examples of functional rules. Families in the later stages of healing have functional rules. They work to make the family stronger. They are a part of the foundation of all healing.

What Roles Do Family Members Develop to Deal With OCD?

Research in the field of family therapy shows that family members behave in predictable ways when they are under stress. Since life in a family under the influence of OCD can be unsettling for both adults and children, family members develop roles as a way to cope and feel more in control. These roles have been given various names by different researchers. Some common roles people learn to play are the responsible one (or hero), the adjuster (or lost one), the placater (or mascot), and the scapegoat (or the person who acts out). In families with OCD, the roles are more rigidly fixed and are enacted with greater compulsion and intensity than in most families.

The "responsible one" is the person in the family who, in order to feel safe, develops a rigid sense of control and says to him/herself, "In the midst of these compulsions and rituals, I'll handle it and take care of it." These people often take over the duties and responsibilities of others, especially those of the person with OCD. They may cover up and protect the person with OCD. These overly responsible people are also referred to as *caretakers*. If this role is adopted by children, they become the super responsible children, often the marvel of their family and the neighborhood.

For example, ten-year-old Marjorie is the oldest child of a family in which her mother continually obsesses that she has run over someone with her car. To keep things more stable, Marjorie takes on a lot of responsibility for managing the family. She often does the laundry, cooks the meals, helps her brothers and sisters with their homework, and makes sure everything is running as smoothly as possible. She seems mature beyond her years and is often praised by family and friends for being such a grown-up young lady.

On the surface, this may seem like a desirable trait, but this sense of over-responsibility is robbing her of a normal childhood. She's always worrying about her mother and father and doesn't have much time to play or to think about her own needs. Unfortunately, while worrying about others, she never has a chance to be a kid, to play with her friends, and to spend time in childhood activities. She pays a price for her role of the "responsible one." She feels cheated, resentful, angry, and socially inept. The "responsible one" might be called the "hero." The hero attempts to make up for the family's weaknesses by super achievement. However, heroes can feel confused and inadequate inside even though they look great outside. (It is critical to distinguish the term "hero" in this context from the use of the term "hero" or "heroine" in their *mythological* sense, which will be described later in the book.)

The "adjuster" attempts to cope with the family's trauma in a different way. The adjuster's guiding thought is, "In the midst of the OCD, I'll ignore it." Feeling powerless in the face of OCD in their parent, spouse, child, or sibling, adjusters cope by detaching, walling themselves off from their feelings and reactions to the unsettling home atmosphere around them. These are people who, in the midst of disturbing and confusing OCD rituals, seem not to notice, continuing their activities no matter what is happening. The person with OCD might be performing rituals and acting irrationally, and the adjuster continues to read, watch TV, or eat dinner as if nothing unusual were going on. Ignoring the irrational behavior of the person with OCD can be a positive way of adapting to the trauma by distancing oneself. For adjusters, however, not noticing becomes a way to dissociate from the feelings of frustration and discomfort they have about the irrational behavior, and their ability to identify and express feelings begins to deteriorate.

Similar to the adjuster is the role of the "lost one" who tries to help or improve things by not being a problem. Like the adjuster, this person makes no demands on anyone and prefers to be a loner. The "lost one," especially if a child, often spends a lot of time alone, playing quietly in his or her room, feeling lonely and forgotten. The lost one pays a price for this coping strategy by feeling unseen and unloved, even irrelevant.

Another role is that of "the placater," whose guiding principle is "In the midst of obsessions and compulsions, I'll fix it and make it better." These people, whether adults or children, try to "fix" or take care of others' feelings, worries, and troubles—everyone's except their own. Placaters in a family with OCD attempt to keep tension and stress levels down by trying to please everybody and often apologize for everything whether it's their fault or not. It's as if they hope this strategy will keep the person with OCD in better control and thus the home environment more comfortable.

Similar to the placater, "the mascot" tries to relieve the tension and lighten up the atmosphere by doing something funny. It's as if mascots try to cover up their pain and confusion with humor and jokes, always performing. The price they pay for this cover-up is a well-developed false self and loss of a real self.

In families with OCD, father or mother might become a "rager," always flying off in an angry tirade in response to something, or an "avoider," refusing to confront or even discuss emotionally challenging issues. Other family members, spouses, or siblings may enable those with OCD by protecting them from threatening situations, covering up for them, or helping them with their rituals. On an episode of "Oprah" dealing with OCD, one woman's fears of contamination were so severe that she was afraid to eat. She insisted that her husband and her mother go through an elaborate series of rituals in order for her to eat anything. The purchase, preparation, and presentation of all her meals had to be carried out in a precise manner or she was too frightened to eat. These exaggerated behaviors exacerbate the formation of unhealthful roles that family members adopt.

Family members under the influence of OCD[24,25] do not choose these roles consciously. They don't sit down and say to themselves, "Our family is in a lot of trouble. I think I'll try to protect myself and make things better by picking a different way to be." These roles are developed unconsciously as a survival technique. Just like the mascot discovers that his humor seems to temporarily distract everyone, other family members stumble on seemingly effective ways to get through life while living in a chaotic and unpredictable atmosphere.

Family members change slowly to adapt to OCD and are often unaware that they've developed rigid ways of reacting and behaving. Only when they become aware of these patterns can they begin to discover and practice new and healthier ways of responding.

Unfortunately, dysfunctional roles can reinforce the unhealthiness of the family and limit the freedom and growth of the individuals. Children who take on such roles often carry them into adulthood and play them out in their own families. For both children and adults, these roles are progressive. Unless interrupted, they become more and more rigid and encompassing, and they affect the atmosphere of the home and its members.

What Effects Do This Family Atmosphere and These Rules and Roles Have Upon the Members?

As you can imagine, these increasingly rigid rules and roles color the atmosphere of the family. Everyone may feel on edge, as if they're walking on egg shells. They may become afraid to try new things. Many family members suffer in silence and isolation, often feeling confused, scared, and bad. They distance themselves from their own feelings and deny their own needs. When they do express a need or say how they feel, the need often doesn't get met, or the expression of feelings just seems to make things worse by fueling the obsessions or compulsions. In fact, they're often blamed for making matters worse. Family members begin to worry that they will say or do something that will somehow "set off" the OCD. The needs and feelings of the person with OCD always seem to come first. Family members become bound by OCD as they restrict their actions and their feelings more and more. The result is a lose-lose situation. Everyone loses: the loved ones and the person with OCD.

Family members often learn to tolerate a multitude of intolerable situations. One family was required to undress on the back porch before they were allowed to enter the house because the person with OCD was terrified of contamination. They all did this without realizing how unreasonable the demand was, and they probably thought that what they were doing would in turn help the person with OCD. In another extreme case, because the person with OCD could not throw out any paper products, family members were forced to sleep outside in the garage as the house was filled with the person's paper "possessions."

In a healthy family, people are free to express what they are feeling, talk about what's happening around them, and grow according to their needs. They are free to organize their lives around their own needs, not solely those of another.

Without help, the illness progresses and the family atmosphere or culture can become increasingly alienating. Rigid rules and roles, while they seem to produce safety, only support the OCD and cripple the loved ones. These rigid and unspoken rules and roles are simply ways to survive the tyranny of OCD by maintaining the status quo, not a way for the family and family members to thrive and grow.

Why Do You Feel Angry, Scared, and Confused So Often?

Because you are human! When you feel wounded—and the effects of OCD on you and your family can be wounding—it is only natural that you would have strong feelings. These feelings can include confusion, sadness, guilt, anger, shame, and fear. These are all normal (ordinary) responses to an abnormal situation. Living with OCD is an abnormal situation when the family system isn't working toward recovery.

At its extreme, the family system is truly suffering. Suffering is endless. It has no beginning, middle, or end. Pain, on the other hand, is limited. It has an onset and an ending. One important task on the journey to recovery is to move from needless suffering to normal pain.

With accurate information, it is possible to begin to understand what is happening in your family. As I stated earlier, ignorance is not bliss. Knowledge is the first step to restoring health. And, as the family moves along the path of recovery, they may experience relief and even exhilaration as they learn to meet the challenge of living with OCD.

Can OCD Become a Family Disorder?

At this point it should be clear to you that OCD can affect not only the person with OCD but also everyone else around this person. It is impossible to live close to someone with OCD without being affected by the illness.[12,13,24,25,59] OCD is a family disorder because the family, like any set of interrelated members or parts, is a system.

In a system, what happens to one part of the system affects all the other parts, just as when one part of a mobile moves, the whole mobile moves. The mobile then seeks to regain its stability. The same is true for any system, even a family. When one member is unhealthy, the whole system may become unhealthy in order to maintain its balance. The support system that once supported the person now supports the disease. For this "balancing act" to end and normalcy to return, everyone in the family system must begin to evaluate whether they are part of the problem or part of the solution.[28]

Just as with OCD, without intervention, the family's way of coping becomes predictable and progressive. As the effects of OCD exact their toll on the OCD sufferer, they also disturb the family atmosphere. The family shame, denial, and enabling behaviors (that para-OCDs develop to "live with the problem") force the family to become isolated and disconnected, not only from each other, but from the community as well. As the OCD gets worse, individual family members, and even friends, can develop stress reactions, health problems, and at times experience economic hardships as a direct result of attempting to cope with OCD.

It has not been long since the major focus in treating OCD was on the primary sufferer. But modern treatment programs clearly show that the family needs its own attention and can recover from its own problems through such activities as individual or family therapy, psychoeducational groups, workshops and seminars, as well as family members' support groups.

Untreated, OCD takes its toll in emotional, physical, and spiritual damage and impacts everyone, even future generations. The key to keeping damage to a minimum is increasing understanding and providing treatment for everyone. With help and support, families can recover from past harm and *prevent* new damage. As we shall discover, families can become even stronger and more powerful through meeting the challenge of living with a person with OCD.

What Is the Disorder That Can Affect the Family Called?

It is no wonder that OCD, like alcoholism and other serious disorders, can create a traumatized family. One of the major lessons learned from the treatment of alcoholism is that the effects extend beyond the person afflicted. The spouses, children, parents, siblings, grandparents, even friends, can all develop emotional, mental, physical, and spiritual reactions. OCD is not only a personal illness, but also a family illness. As mentioned earlier, I call the characteristic behaviors and symptoms that the family and other loved ones under the influence of OCD display "para-OCDism."

These "para-OCDs" are affected by their own disorder, one with its own onset, treatment, and outcome. Para-OCDism, like co-alcoholism or codependence, is the parallel disorder that strikes those under the influence of OCD. This para-OCDism remarkably resembles the old concept called codependence from the alcoholism field. Codependence was typically described as loss of one's self to another person, place, or thing.[5]

Para-OCDism unfolds as family members make an effort to adapt in a family that tries to protect the person with OCD and thereby inadvertently enables the person with OCD to engage in his or her compulsions and rituals. OCD family expert Marlene Cooper, in her work with families with OCD, also notes this similarity to codependence. She states, "This enabling or colluding in provocative behaviors resembles the struggle that occurs in alcoholic families and has led us to look at how OCD families become co-dependent in their loved one's illness."[13]

As we have seen, the family atmosphere in these homes is typically crisis-oriented, especially those struggling with the more severe and undiagnosed cases. No one can relax. Danger is seen everywhere. No one knows when, where, or how the OCD will be triggered. The family continually remains on "red alert," contouring its behavior around the illness. This is para-OCDism. Just as there are many more people with OCD than originally thought, there are a large number of unrecognized and untreated people who suffer from this parallel disorder.

How Many Para-OCDs Are There?

It is often estimated that four to six people are directly affected by each person with a major illness.[27] Researcher and author Judith Rapoport estimated that more than four million people suffer from OCD. We now believe the number is much higher, with possibly seven-and-a-half to eight million people struggling with OCD. If other problems related to OCD are included—e.g., depression, anxiety, sleep disturbances, panic disorders like agoraphobia, other phobias, hair pulling (trichotillomania) and even some forms of eating disorders—the number may be even higher. With four to six people affected by one person with OCD, then there may be anywhere between sixteen million and forty-eight million "para-OCDs." While the term para-OCD is still being defined, it gives the family and other loved ones a term to describe their experiences, at least for now.

Will Everybody Develop Problems?

Not every individual living with an OCD sufferer will develop related problems severe enough to require professional attention, although everyone is affected.[24,25] Whether one develops problems or not depends on a complex interaction between the type and severity of the OCD, the temperament and acquired characteristics of those close to the sufferer, and the environmental support available to both the person with OCD and the loved ones.

Some families may have sufficient resources and resiliencies, and they remain relatively unaffected by the OCD. With no help, however, family members may exhibit one or more of a variety of symptoms. Conversely, OCD can be a crucible for the development of excellence— a testing ground from which you and your family emerge stronger and with new strengths and clearer vision.

There are common issues with which para-OCDs may have to grapple. Certainly not all of these characteristics occur. I'll describe these common problems in the chapter on "Core Issues," so you will know what to watch for in yourself and your family.

How Are Different Family Members Affected?

Everyone in a family under the influence of OCD is exposed to ongoing, albeit intermittent, traumatizing circumstances. The severity of the trauma can vary across families and even within families at different points in the family's development. Both the severity and frequency of the OCD symptoms can vary within and across families. Furthermore, the resources available to each family differ. Nevertheless, two truisms stand out: each person is affected, and no two people are affected in exactly the same way. Yet, some useful generalizations do exist about OCD's different impact on family members.

When one or more parents have OCD, the children are exposed to a double dose of trauma: OCD and the loss of parenting. First, the loss of one parent, let alone the loss of both parents, may be one of the greatest traumas a person can incur. Further, this large wound is accompanied by a strong dose of embarrassment, shame, guilt, and blame. These children may suffer from developmental delays as well as low self-esteem. When these children grow up, the now-adult children once again may feel called upon to shoulder the responsibility of caring for the aging parent. These adult children may feel angry and resentful that they were not nurtured by a parent for whom they now feel a caring obligation.

When a child has OCD, parents also get a double dose of trauma. They feel guilty because they can't heal or even protect their child. They may worry feverishly about the future and constantly wonder what will happen to their adult child with OCD after they are gone. To compound the situation, parents frequently have opposing views on what is best for the child and the family. Their relationship can become a casualty of OCD. On the other hand, their relationship can flourish with appropriate support and become an inspiration to others.

When a spouse, or life partner, develops OCD, the loss and separation can reach profound depths. There may be periods of great inequality because one member can become so impaired by OCD that he or she is unable to leave the house, go to work, or experience respite, let alone peace of mind. Sexuality is often an arena tinged with fear, caution, and lots of hurt feelings. If the person with OCD has contamination fears, for example, that person may not want to catch or give any diseases and therefore withdraws from sexual relations. This proves damaging and confusing to both the person with OCD and his or her significant other.

When a sibling has OCD, the brothers and sisters incur their own separate and unique wounds. With increasing focus on the OCD member, siblings miss out on parenting and suffer parental loss. They are also prone to feel "survivor's guilt." This is the reaction described in the trauma literature which attests to the extreme guilt of those who witness a traumatic event, but are not killed or hurt themselves. Siblings often cope with this reaction by distancing themselves from their brother or sister, avoiding the person with OCD, or escaping from the home altogether.

When a grandchild has OCD, the feelings of helplessness may invite despair. Watching a grandchild live in fear and agony can be frightening.

Seeing the ones you love most in the world—your children and your grandchildren—suffer can be heart-wrenching. The result can create conflict between parents and grandparents and distance the grandparents from other grandchildren.

When a friend has OCD, loved ones may feel confused about the OCD sufferer's behavior and be unsure about the appropriateness of discussing their observations and confusion with the friend's family. Friends often sit and watch helplessly, too, as their companions become more and more engulfed by this strange disorder.

As always, healthy, open, and frank discussions about the illness and its effects on everyone can be a helpful and healing experience for all. If discussions prove difficult, written materials about OCD may be beneficial.

What Are Some of the Warning Signs of Para-OCD?

In general, not taking care of yourself, physically, emotionally, and spiritually, are signs of para-OCD. One of the most indicative signs is burnout. You may feel used up by the time and energy it takes to deal with the presence of OCD in your life. You may have been caring for others for so long that you feel like you have nothing left to give.

Another signpost of para-OCD is that you find yourself spending almost as much time worrying and obsessing about the person with OCD as the person with OCD spends on their obsessions and rituals. As a result, you and your family, including the member with OCD, may become increasingly unable to participate in everyday activities. You make decisions about what you can and cannot do based on whether the OCD will be accommodating.

You also may feel anxious, nervous, frightened, angry, resentful, exhausted, or guilty. And you could suffer from a variety of stress-related disorders, such as headaches, gastrointestinal problems, anxiety, or depression. You might also find yourself trying to cope by overeating, using alcohol, additional drugs, or other potentially addictive substances to numb your feelings. These feelings, stress-related disorders, and addictive behaviors may be warning signs that you and other family members are experiencing para-OCDism.

What Happens Over Time to the Para-OCD Sufferer?

Without recovery, the para-OCD sufferer's symptoms tend to worsen, just as the OCD sufferer's symptoms often worsen with time unless they are in a recovery process. The family disorder may also be progressive. Although there is a waxing and waning nature to OCD, usually time does not heal either the OCD or the para-OCDism that affects the family. Roles, rules, and behaviors get more firmly entrenched and become more difficult for family members to recognize and to change.

What might have seemed abnormal and bizarre when the symptoms of OCD began can become more and more "natural" as time goes on. Undressing on the back porch, retracing the family's route in the car to check for injured or dead bodies, washing for hours on end, endlessly checking the windows—all these unnecessary and illogical rituals tend to increase over time, yet they become more and more accepted as part of who your family is and what it does. All the strange and senseless behaviors required of you become accepted and the OCD and para-OCDism worsen. Untreated, your tolerance for illogical, unnecessary, and bizarre behavior increases. Also, the core emotional issues, which you'll learn about in Chapter Four, can worsen. Treated, you and your family can heal, regain health, and become stronger.

What Effects Do the Length of Time Under the Influence of OCD Have on the Family System?

The length of time one lives with OCD does have an impact. Without treatment, the rules, roles, and unhealthy accommodating behaviors continue to become more fixed and more difficult to interrupt. That is why early diagnosis and treatment are vitally important for both the OCD sufferer and the family members. Once healing begins, however, much can be done to restore the happiness and overall healthy functioning of the family. The length of time of living with OCD has less effect when the family and loved ones are motivated to change.

There is an old expression: "It's not how long it takes you to get there, but what you do once you are there that counts." The same is true in a family affected by OCD.

What Needs to Occur in Order for the Family to Recover?

First, and foremost, the family needs to know what they're dealing with. Lack of knowledge prevents people from beginning their recovery. In order to recover, you have to know that the person you love has OCD and what that means. Having a person with OCD in the house can be like having an elephant in the living room. Everyone sees it and knows that it's there, but no one says anything about it or knows what to do about it. Family members step around the elephant and pretend not to see it. Most of all, they don't talk about it. Everyone in the family needs to know that this "elephant" is OCD, and they must be allowed to see it and talk about it. You and all the other loved ones of the person with OCD need to know how OCD can change families and how to work to undo the harmful effects of this uninvited intruder.

Once you understand that the elephant in your living room is OCD, you can get help in a variety of ways. This help can range from self-help books to professional help. While knowledge is important in dealing with OCD, reading a book is usually not enough. For some, Obsessive-Compulsive Anonymous (OCA) is enough. Millions of families of alcoholics have found support and recovery in Al-Anon. Many family members of people with OCD have found the same healing touch in OCA. While OCA is primarily a program for people with OCD, family members are welcome at open OCA meetings.

How Do Para-OCDs Begin Their Recovery?

If you are the family or loved one of a person with OCD, you have already begun your recovery by coming as far as you have now. You have already bitten into the apple and your desire for knowledge can continue to grow.

You begin your healing by understanding that there is a serious illness affecting a person you love and, even more importantly, affecting you. Next, learn all you can about this disease. Get outside help if you have any question about whether you are under the influence of OCD. Set limits with the person with OCD that allow for your needs as well as the needs of the person with OCD. As difficult as it may seem, a necessary step is to accept that you can't do anything directly about the obsessions and compulsions. Fortunately, you can do a great deal about the effect that OCD has on you.

OCD can be likened to a wind that blows through the family. You can't see the wind, but you can clearly feel its effects. It can be like a gentle breeze, barely rustling the leaves or disturbing the surface of the water. Or, it can swoop through like a tornado and topple the house. In a home where OCD is shrouded in secrecy and shame, the wind can continue to blow everything down because secrecy and shame make a weak structure. When OCD is acknowledged and understood, however, the wind can blow, but the house will stand. If the structure is made of the right materials, the wind can simply pass through and actually enhance one's mastery over one of nature's forces, like a tree that develops strength because of the wind's buffeting.

Like the wind, the atmosphere in a family with OCD varies depending on the stage of awareness and healing in which the family finds itself. As you and your family move through the stages of recovery, the atmosphere in your home can change for the better. There is much to be hopeful about in the twenty-first century. Knowledge and support can be life savers. Just as a life preserver thrown to a drowning person can save that person's life, there are life preservers for OCD family members. You don't have to feel like you're drowning.

—⟋⟍—

CHAPTER 3

Becoming Aware—
The Great Discovery

—⚋—

What Is "The Great Discovery"?

When you become aware of the physical, emotional, spiritual, and possible genetic vulnerabilities that you as a family member or loved one acquire as a result of being under the influence of OCD, you begin your healing. Just as the person with OCD discovers, "It's not me; it's the OCD," you, too, make a parallel discovery, "It's not you; it's the OCD." And just as this crucial discovery helps the OCD sufferer, your great discovery becomes the gateway to your recovery. It can lead you to a recognition of your own wounds and to your own journey of healing.

It's easy to underestimate the importance of this discovery. Knowing what you are dealing with isn't so easy! A recent consensus of experts found that, on average, people with OCD see three to four doctors and spend more than nine years seeking treatment before they receive a correct diagnosis. Furthermore, experts[36] found that it takes an average of seventeen years from the time OCD begins to get appropriate help.

The discovery that your loved one has OCD can either hit like a bolt of lightning when you get the diagnosis or be the result of a gradual awareness and acceptance emerging over the course of the disorder. The diagnosis can lead to very useful discoveries. For example, you find that you are not alone. You find that you are not crazy. You find that you did not cause the OCD, and you are not responsible for curing it. You find that you cannot control it either. But most importantly, you find that you can cope with it regardless of what the person with OCD does. You learn to work smarter, not necessarily harder, at dealing with the impact of OCD on your life. That's a lot more to remember than first appears. It is important to remind yourself every day of each and every one of these discoveries, especially early in your healing and recovery.

Once you recognize that there is an understandable, diagnosable, and treatable problem with which the person you love is afflicted, your denial stops. Energy is released as you no longer have to pretend or suffer in ignorance or isolation. The energy you once used to block out feelings and maintain false beliefs can now be used in the service of your freedom. Remember philosopher Jean-Paul Sartre's definition, "Freedom is what we do with what's been done to us."

How Can You Become More Aware?

Becoming more aware picks up momentum as you recognize who has what problem. Yes, those with OCD have a neurophysiological disorder. You, the family member, intimate, and/or loved one, can have a parallel problem of your own that results in a clearly described syndrome or group of symptoms.

Becoming educated about OCD and its influence on others is the key to becoming aware. Reading this book may be the first important step in becoming aware of the nature of OCD and the vulnerabilities you may have acquired by loving someone with OCD and living under its influence. In addition to this book, becoming more aware might include reading other books, listening to tapes, attending lectures, reading articles, watching special OCD films[9,10] such as James Callner's

"The Touching Tree" or "The Risk," consulting knowledgeable professionals, attending support groups, and allowing yourself to be open to all of the information that is emerging about OCD.

One of the better sources of help is Obsessive-Compulsive Anonymous (OCA).[45] This 12-Step program is designed for persons with OCD to come together to share their experience, strength, and hope. Although specifically designed for those who have OCD, you may find others there who share many of your concerns and experiences. It's so important to feel heard and supported and to know you're not alone, both for the person with OCD and for the family members. Finding a group of people who understand and share your experience can be freeing and empowering.

In a chapter titled *"To Our Families and Friends"* in the "Big Book," *OCA: Recovering from Obsessive-Compulsive Disorder,* it says, "Living with or being close to someone with OCD can be every bit as difficult as having the problem itself." It describes the family's "enabling" environment that unwittingly fosters the self-destructive obsessions and compulsions of the sufferer. It also emphasizes the need of the family to "detach," so that family members can heal regardless of what happens to the person with OCD.

It is likely that, in the near future, there will be an OC-Anon in your community for family and friends of the person with OCD. Just as Al-Anon followed on the heels of AA, the time seems ripe for the formation of a para-OCD anonymous program, a self-help fellowship for the family, loved ones, and friends of those with OCD. Until those groups form, you can learn a great deal and get needed support in OCA. If there are no OCA meetings in your area, you might try other 12-Step meetings that deal with similar issues such as Codependents Anonymous (CODA) or Adult Children of Alcoholics (ACOA).

The OC Foundation, the national organization for OCD sufferers and their families, is a valuable resource for information and support. The Foundation distributes information about OCD by newsletters and tapes. They hold annual conferences in the United States where people with OCD from all over the world and their loved ones gather to share information and to support each other. Workshops at these conferences are designed for family members and others to provide information about how to deal with OCD.

In addition to OCA, the OC Foundation, and other support groups, you may decide that counseling would be helpful for you and for your family. Finding an individual therapist may be an important first step on this journey to recovery. You may want and need many members on your team—an individual therapist skilled in working with stressed individuals and families, a good physician for both yourself and the person with OCD, a member of the clergy to help address the possibility of spiritual wounding, as well as group support such as OCA.

Think of these people and organizations as part of a team of players, in this case your external support team. It may also be helpful for you to begin to identify and assemble an *internal* team of players—different parts of yourself that you can recognize, develop, and call upon in different situations. For instance, you might begin to work on a part of yourself that is knowledgeable and skilled with dealing with the person with OCD when they are obsessing and performing rituals. You might also recognize and honor your loving, empathetic side that can be useful when someone in your family needs love and nurturing. There might also be a part of this internal team that is responsible for protecting you and caring for your own needs. Each of us needs all the help we can get in this journey of life, and it's important to assemble and develop both external and internal teams.

Another increasingly helpful resource for families under the influence of OCD is the Journey of Hope (JOH),[3,4] a National Alliance for the Mentally Ill (NAMI) membership service that provides family education and self-help support to families and friends of those who have been diagnosed with a mental illness. During this group's initial formation in 1979, the families of people with schizophrenia formed most of its constituents. Soon, the families of those with bipolar disorder began coming, then families of those suffering depression. Most recently, especially on the East Coast, families of those afflicted by OCD are joining and finding relief, comfort, and healing.

Currently, JOH has affiliations in more than thirty-five states and two provinces in Canada. It provides an invaluable service to those affected by mental illness, including OCD. Believing in the importance of acknowledging and using the concept of a higher power, it advocates "The Ten Principles of Support" that are transforming the lives of families everywhere. Further discussion of JOH appears later in this book.

In the late 1990s, an organization called The Awareness Foundation for OCD & Related Disorders was formed. A nonprofit Charitable Foundation, its board of directors features some of the world's most respected professionals on OCD. The Awareness Foundation provides professional presentations and speakers who are available to provide workshops, in-services, consultations, and seminars to parents and students, community groups, school personnel, healthcare providers, and professional organizations.

All the knowledge that you can gain from these resources arms you in your struggle with OCD. Unchecked, OCD can be like a shredder, consuming everything in its path. As is true in most instances, forewarned is forearmed. It's important in this encounter, though, to remember who the enemy is. This battle you're arming yourself for is with the illness of OCD and not with the person with OCD. This is a critical distinction to keep in mind. The clearer the distinction between the illness of OCD and the person with OCD, the better you will be able to help yourself, your family, and the person with OCD. It may be helpful to view the OCD as a separate, undeserved, and uninvited part of your loved one. The person with OCD did not choose OCD or want to have this problem any more than you do.

Have You Been Traumatized Also?

Trauma occurs in all families that have a member under the influence of a major illness. OCD is no exception. You, too, may have been wounded by this disease, just as the person with OCD has been. The word trauma comes from the Greek *tramaticos,* or wound. The most common definition of trauma is "a physical wound." As we've seen, wounds can be stress-related illnesses like migraines, sleep disorders, or gastrointestinal problems. These are all physical wounds one can incur living under the influence of chronic stress.

The wounding that occurs in families with OCD can also be of a second kind, which the *American Heritage Dictionary* lists as "an emotional shock that [can] create substantial and lasting damage to the psychological development of the individual." Trauma can be further defined as "something that severely jars the mind and emotions." OCD can certainly jar the mind, the emotions, the soul, and the spirit. The effect of trauma on the body is usually more obvious than the effect on the mind and emotions. Trauma, however, can create just as deep a wounding to the emotional and nonmaterial body.

A family under the influence of OCD can be affected from four sources of trauma that correspond roughly to the four characteristics of the family culture: *traumatic stress,* from the uncertainty, unpredictability, arbitrariness, and chaos of the compulsions and obsessions; *traumatic loss,* from the lost potential of the loved one, as well as the loss of having to give up so many important things of your own; *traumatic grief,* from being unable to share and express the pains and hurts caused by the OCD; and *traumatic exhaustion,* from caring for and reacting to the OCD sufferer.

There can also be abuse of all types in families affected by OCD. You may feel like you have to pick up the slack for your family member with OCD and do the work that the person doesn't, can't, or won't do. It may also be difficult to find the time and energy to devote to your own goals and life when you're preoccupied with caring for another with OCD. Hearing a litany of complaints about what you are doing or not doing, or being the butt of anger because you no longer participate in compulsive rituals is also abusive.

Why Do You Do All the Wrong Things When You Try to Help?

In trying to help the person with OCD, you may find you frequently end up doing things that appear to make the OCD worse. Initially, this can be frustrating and confusing, but later it can become a source of anger and resentment. In trying to make things easier for the person with OCD, and make family life less chaotic and more controllable, you may find yourself accommodating or "helping" the person with OCD by checking the doors and locks for him or her, or by offering repeated assurances, or by answering endless questions, all of which seem to make the OCD sufferer feel worse. In the case of OCD, doing what initially or at first glance seems kind or helpful may often be precisely the wrong approach. Thinking that you're being helpful, you may do all the wrong things for the right reasons. In the example of "offering repeated assurances," the right response for the family member would be to stop answering questions and giving assurance.

Another challenge can occur when you begin trying to do the appropriate things. Because you are no longer participating in compulsions and rituals, or enabling the person with OCD, he or she may become angry with you. The person with OCD may accuse you of being cruel, insensitive, unhelpful, or simply trying to make things worse. People with OCD often try to convince you that doing what they want is the only way for them to feel better, and they may be quite insistent and persistent. You may feel stuck between a rock and a hard place.

Janet Greeson, author and mother of a child with OCD, says, "Our compassion for our loved one could be the very thing that prolongs the illness." It's not unlike families who enable alcoholics. By "fixing" the problems, they become a part of the problem. It's natural to be compassionate. The dilemma for family members is trying to figure out the rightness of your actions. Following the principles in this book can help you heal or recover yourself.

What Is the Process of Healing?

Dr. Elizabeth Kubler-Ross, a psychiatrist who spent much of her professional life working closely with dying patients and their families, noticed that they often experienced five stages when faced with illness and impending death. The universality of these stages can apply to you also. You may experience some or all of these stages in your healing from the trauma of the OCD.

The first stage is usually *Denial*. We've seen how dangerous denial can be. Kubler-Ross observed that when people stop denying the problem and begin to recognize and acknowledge what is happening to them, they frequently go through a second stage called *Bargaining*. In this second stage, people try to "make deals" with God or the universe. Children are particularly susceptible to this sort of magical thinking. They may promise to do or not do certain things in the belief that they can strike a bargain with some unseen force to make the problem go away. For example, a child whose father has OCD may tell God that she will be very good, always keep her room clean, and never be mean to her little brother if only God will let Daddy feel better. It's natural to engage in bargaining when faced with threatening situations. In fact, this bargaining can be strikingly similar to some of the rituals of the person with OCD. How many times have you, the family member, thought, "Maybe if I do this, then that won't happen?"

When you find that bargaining does not change the OCD, you might move to the next stage, *Anger*. Now that you can admit how much OCD is affecting you and your loved ones, you may become angry at the injustice of the OCD itself, the person with OCD, yourself, the world, and even God. You may feel furious and then guilty and ashamed for having these feelings about someone who is sick. This, however, is an understandable, human response to the roller-coaster ride that dealing with OCD takes you on.

When the full reality of what you're dealing with finally sets in, a period of *Depression* can follow. You see no way out and don't know where to turn for help. You may feel hopeless and helpless against what may seem like insurmountable obstacles in your life.

Once you can cope with all of these feelings without condemning yourself or the person with OCD, you enter the last stage called *Acceptance*. Typically spiritual, this stage is characterized by a lack of resistance to circumstances as they are. No longer is energy spent fighting against what is and chasing what can't be. This does not necessarily mean moving away from the person with OCD, but rather moving away from your obsession with the illness. With acceptance you become free to plan ways to help yourself and your family.

Other writers have recognized and described these stages. While some of the words are different, the process is universal. Quoting from *Al-Anon Faces Alcoholism,* Roy C. describes the progression in this way: Denial, Adjustment Techniques, Attempting to Eliminate the Problem, Restructuring Within the Problem, which lead to a hoped-for stage of Recovery and Reorganization.[6]

Regardless of how you describe this process of adjusting to OCD in your life, you can learn that how *you* respond to the challenge of this illness is the key to living and making peace with it! We often have little control over events that occur in life, but we have a great deal of control over our responses to them.

What Responsibility Does the Person With OCD Have?

OCD is a treatable disorder, and many with OCD symptoms need to seek treatment. They have the responsibility to get help. No one else can do that for them. Remember the old saying, "You can lead a horse to water, but you can't make him drink." While that may be true, you can help to make the horse thirsty. There may be ways you can influence the person with OCD to seek treatment—first, by requiring the person to assume responsibility for himself or herself in a manner consistent with his or her abilities or, secondly, by refusing to participate in the person's obsessions or compulsions.

But in the final analysis, those with OCD are responsible for their own recovery. People with OCD also have the same responsibilities as the rest of us. But because they do have OCD, they have to take care of themselves in special ways. It's no different than if they had any other chronic illness, like diabetes, for example. They would need to learn what they must do to be as healthy and productive as possible. There are special ways that people with OCD need to care for themselves, and, much of the time, it is up to them to find out what these ways are and to follow through with their treatment. There are times, however, when OCD sufferers are so entwined in their illness that they are unable to act in a responsible manner and may need to be in a structured day-treatment center or even a hospital.

What Can You Do About OCD?

If what you mean by this question is "Can I change the OCD?" the answer is "No." Only the person with OCD can enter treatment and change the course of his or her illness. You can, however, change yourself and your reaction to this disorder. Paradoxically, this may have a powerful effect on the course of the OCD. So, the two initial questions are "How do I do this?" and "How do I get started?"

First, accept the reality that your loved one has a disorder. Denying it, ignoring it, or minimizing it rarely helps. We cannot respond in a meaningful way to what we aren't aware of. Acceptance of the disorder is the first step. The second step is to take care of yourself. You have probably placed your needs after those of the person with OCD. You need to change your focus and begin to use your energy to care for yourself first. Remember the airplane metaphor—"Secure your oxygen mask before helping others!" Taking care of yourself, and encouraging other family members to do the same, helps to ensure that you are able to help other family members when appropriately needed. Unless you take care of yourself and stay physically, emotionally, mentally, and spiritually healthy, you won't be able to help yourself, your family, or the person with OCD.

Establish appropriate boundaries between yourself and others in the family, especially between yourself and the person with OCD. In *Boundaries: Where You End and I Begin,* therapist and author Anne Katherine[37] suggests, "Good boundaries allow us to be close to others without losing ourselves." A person with good boundaries knows he or she is not responsible for someone else's feelings or behaviors. Establishing and maintaining adequate and useful boundaries are particularly important skills for families with OCD to learn and practice because OCD tends to encroach on everyone's lives.

Setting limits and establishing boundaries are healthy and appropriate aspects of keeping your boundaries intact. You might decide, for example, just how much you're willing to listen to the person with OCD ruminate and obsess and how much you're willing to participate in his or her rituals and compulsions. Studies show that up to 80 percent of family members participate in or accommodate OCD.[62]

Normalize your life and your family's life as much as possible. You may have stopped doing certain things because of the OCD. Experiment with new behaviors. Do things by yourself and with your family, and encourage the person with OCD to do likewise. Strive for compassion for the suffering of the person with OCD, and also make a commitment to your own life and interests. In the long run, this helps everyone.

Get help when you need it. The stress on family members can be enormous. Reach out to others, including extended family, friends, therapists, and support groups. People with OCD are often isolated because of fear and shame. Family members may become isolated too. Caring support and competent help can make a world of difference.

Roy C.[6] emphasizes the importance of "learning about OCD, experiencing and expressing feelings, taking action, making choices, getting our needs met, and letting go of unrealistic expectations of the person with OCD as well as perfectionist standards for ourselves." With practice you can learn to say "No," create healthy boundaries, take more time for enjoyment, and honor your own needs, even if they aren't as dramatic as those of the person with OCD. While these steps may seem like small efforts in the face of such a large problem, they will have a powerful and positive effect on your life, your family's well-being, and ultimately, the health of your loved one.

What Feelings Can You Expect at This Stage?

The process of becoming aware can be like coming out of anesthesia when, as you regain consciousness, you become aware of many things. As you become more aware of OCD's impact on your life, you can expect to have a wide variety of feelings. This is normal, natural, and necessary. You may, at times, feel all the emotions mentioned earlier, such as frustration, anger, sadness, grief, guilt, fear, joy, relief, hope, and more. No matter how well you learn to cope with this disorder, you're bound at times to feel "bad, sick, crazy, and dumb"[27] yourself because OCD can make you feel crazy at times.

Feeling these emotions is a clear sign that you are beginning to allow yourself to experience denied or buried emotions. Congratulations!

This is progress! If feelings have been repressed or not acknowledged, they may have built up pressure that needs to be released. It's as if a covered pot of water has been boiling on the stove and building up pressure. Once the lid is removed, there is an initial burst of steam, but as the pressure is released, the boiling is reduced. The same is true with your feelings. If they have been repressed, or not acknowledged for a long time, they may have built up considerable pressure that needs to be released, perhaps slowly.

Learn to relate to OCD as if it were a foreign intruder or separate entity. To develop the distinction that OCD is separate from the one you love, you can distance OCD from the person by giving it a name like "Mr. OCD," "Mr. Worry," "Oscar the OCD bug," or "The Monster." You may get to the point where you both can fight the OCD on one hand and accept it on the other. You can develop many tools to learn how to do battle and to learn acceptance. Remember, there are a thousand things you can't do and a thousand things you can do for yourself and the person with OCD.

What Do You Do With Your Feelings of Shame, Guilt, Disgust, Despair, Depression, and Anger?

First, allow yourself the dignity of your own feelings. You can no more control your feelings than OCD sufferers can control their obsessions or compulsions. Learn to accept them as evidence of your humanity. These feelings are common and normal for any person or family dealing with a serious illness. It would be very unusual for you not to have feelings in a circumstance such as dealing with OCD.

It is also common for loved ones to feel guilty for sharing the family's secrets with others or guilty that they're not sick too. The thinking goes something like this, "How can I complain about my life when the person with OCD seems to be suffering so?" or "What right do I have to talk about something that my loved one considers confidential, personal, or private?" Additionally, you may feel ashamed of the person with OCD or ashamed of your own reactions. Anger at the person with OCD and the illness itself as well as its effect on your family is understandable. Depression and despair are also common feelings during this stage of your recovery.

The next key to dealing with all these feelings is to do something with them. It is not helpful to suffer alone and in silence. Seek help and support, talk to others, read self-help books about how others have dealt with similar feelings, go to support groups, get treatment.

It may be helpful to think of your life as a plate. If you have a fifty-cent-size portion of peas on your plate and the plate is small, the peas fill most of the plate. If the plate is twice as big, however, the peas take up half the space and the amount of peas looks smaller. Making your plate bigger, by taking a walk, visiting a friend, or going to a movie, for example, can be of great help. The problem, in this case OCD, stays the same in terms of how big it is, but it becomes smaller and smaller when the playing field becomes larger and larger. We'll talk more later about how to make your plate bigger.

What Do You Do With Your Resentment Toward the Person With OCD?

John has OCD. He doesn't work; he doesn't clean his room; he just sits around and obsesses. If John were your son, you might feel resentful because you feel taken advantage of. If John were your husband, you might feel resentment because you have to bear the financial responsibility for the family and do most of the parenting. If John were your brother, you might be resentful because he gets away with things you can't get away with. If John were a friend, you might not be able to depend on him.

When the anger that you feel toward the OCD and the person with OCD is not expressed, it can lead to resentment. Resentment is the result of feeling angry over and over again. Dictionaries often define anger as a feeling of displeasure and indignation stemming from a sense of being injured or offended. You may feel injured or offended by the unpredictable behavior and unreasonable demands of the person with OCD. You've probably spent a lot of time and energy taking care of others, particularly the person with OCD, at the expense of your own needs.

The best way to deal with your resentment is to acknowledge that it's there, and to acknowledge that it is understandable that you would feel this way. Be loving and forgiving with yourself. Let yourself off the hook. Feelings are nothing to be ashamed of. Look for a way to express your anger so it doesn't build and turn into resentment or turn inward into depression and despair. It can be helpful to express it to the OCD sufferer, and you might also need to express it and get it off your chest by talking with someone else. Yet another way to express your anger might be to channel it into constructive behaviors like exercise or work.

When anger is dealt with in healthy ways, you will still feel the anger but you'll be able to express it and get through it. When it's acknowledged and accepted, you can get over anger. Unacknowledged and unaccepted, anger can turn into resentment that seems to last forever. Resentment is more of a state of consciousness and fills up whatever space is available. It can color your entire relationship with the person with OCD and others. By dealing with your anger, you will free yourself from resentment's poisonous cloud and fallout.

How Do You Know If You Need More Help?

You need more help when you find yourself or other family members having trouble in the following areas: social, business, financial, or legal; and when, in the words of Roy C., "caring becomes guilt, over-sacrifice and a feeling of being consumed or burnt out by someone else's illness." If this happens, you may need help in working through these problems and coming up with new plans and strategies. If you're spending more time worrying about and taking care of the person with OCD than yourself, you may need help. Signs of severe stress could be the variety of emotional and physical symptoms mentioned earlier. The stress of living with a person with OCD, or someone with any major illness, can be managed with help. You can learn to do more than just survive; you can even flourish in stressful situations. People often need professional help when faced with difficult life circumstances. Don't deny yourself this help when it seems appropriate.

How Do You Choose a Therapist?

Ask the prospective therapist if he or she knows about OCD and understands how OCD affects the family. As Roy C. wisely advises "Find a therapist who will talk about you and not just the person with OCD." The therapist should understand how illness in general, and OCD in particular, can affect a family and should be familiar with the atmosphere, rules, and roles family members develop in order to cope. If the therapist you choose doesn't know about OCD, he or she could do all of the wrong things for the right reasons and could be damaging in the process. For example, the therapist might spend time analyzing willpower or the underlying dynamics of the person with OCD and, consequently, that focus could lead to putting expectations on the person with OCD that can never be achieved.

Interview several therapists. Do not be afraid to ask a lot of questions and trust your impressions and feelings about both the person's knowledge and your ability to feel safe and comfortable. Therapy can also be thought of as a journey, and the relationship that you and your family establish with a therapist is critical. You would be wise to choose someone knowledgeable, loving, and even tough. As one of my clients said, look for "an S.O.B. with a heart."

What Are the Pitfalls of This Stage?

In this stage of your recovery, it is important to move slowly as you become aware of the challenges that you face. It's important to share your strength, hope, and pain with others and to be aware of the tendency to attribute either all or none of life's troubles to OCD. Neither extreme is helpful. I know of people who have used their increased awareness of the effects of OCD on their families as an excuse for every problem they have. For example, James blames all of his financial problems on his son who is in treatment for OCD and requires therapy and medication. Oliver blames his wife Martha, who has OCD, for his career indecisiveness, believing that the time and attention he gives to her illness is the primary reason he hasn't been able to develop his career.

Good advice is to slow down, take your time, and be gentle with yourself. Even while reading this book, you can practice taking your time and taking care of yourself. Learning is much more powerful and lasting when it is spread out over time. Stop and think about how much you've learned already. Congratulate yourself on the distance you have already covered. If you are having trouble with these beginning steps, it might be useful to seek help from one of the resources I have mentioned (see Appendix A), or from a professional therapist.

What Happens as a Result of Family Awareness?

Family awareness can become the gateway to recovery. The increased awareness of OCD and its possible effects leads you to reflect on what you have been doing and examine the helpfulness or harmfulness of your current behaviors. From this new vantage point, you have an opportunity to begin identifying your own issues and the problems that you may be grappling with as you try to deal with the impact of OCD. These ways of reacting to OCD are probably hurting you and your family. As painful as the struggle can be, OCD leads you to your own issues—and dealing with your own issues leads you into your recovery. There is work ahead as you deal with these core issues, but there is help and hope ahead as well.

—ɷ—

CHAPTER 4

Identifying Your Issues— The Fallout of Living Under the Influence of OCD

—〰—

What Happens to Family Members Under the Influence of OCD Without a Recovery Program?

Widely different results are possible when we live under the influence of OCD. What happens to family members depends not only on the severity of the OCD, but even more importantly on their reactions and responses to the OCD and their reactions and responses to the person with the OCD. When neither the person with OCD nor the family and loved ones are in recovery, they are all apt to show a host of symptoms of varying degrees: physically, emotionally, behaviorally and spiritually. They may develop psychosomatic problems, which are real physical illnesses with an emotional origin. In the emotional realm, they may experience depression as they narrow or limit their attention to the OCD, or they may feel anxious and tense because of the ever-present threat of the OCD. Behaviorally, families can fall apart or move apart, members can become addicted to drugs (or work, food, sex, or money), or members can become abusive to themselves or others in other ways. On a spiritual level, family members may lose a sense of meaning, purpose, or vision in life, and retreat from the refuge of spirituality.

What Happens to Family Members Under the Influence of OCD With a Recovery Program?

At the other end of the recovery spectrum, both the person with OCD and the loved ones seek recovery and healing. They both learn about the nature and course of the disorder and its far-reaching impact; they seek treatment; and they actively involve themselves in a healing program to address the physical, emotional, and spiritual damage in their lives. Only after the influence of the OCD is acknowledged are members ready to deal with the personal issues that beset them.

Although there is ongoing stress and loss in the family—whether it involves the loss of relationship, dream, hope, or financial resources—life can be manageable even in the presence of OCD. In fact, the very challenge of OCD can propel everyone in the family to higher levels of growth. The family can actually be "weller than well" in 12-Step parlance.

There are variations of this scenario, where either the individual with OCD or the loved one(s) is in a recovery process and the other person isn't. It is critical to remember that the person with OCD does not need to be in treatment or recovery in order for other members of the family to heal, although it certainly makes life easier and more pleasant. While it is desirable that everyone be working and growing together, it is not essential. Families living with OCD can become strong and whole in spite of the OCD because they are working to improve their ability to live with OCD.

What Kinds of Personal Consequences Might You Incur Living Under the Influence of OCD?

I have found that there are generally three sets of issues that families and loved ones experience when under the influence of OCD.[24,25]

While these issues can show up at any time, it is useful to think of them as unfolding over time. The first set of issues stems primarily from the trauma of the OCD. These issues usually appear first, although they can resurface again and again just as OCD can wax and wane. The second set of issues stems from an ever-present sense of loss that accompanies OCD. They usually show up after family members have adapted to the OCD symptoms. The third set of issues inevitably stems from prolonged exposure to OCD.

What Is the First Set of Issues That the Family and Loved Ones Face in the Progression of OCD?

The first set of common issues involves methods of coping with the trauma of living with OCD, and these issues emerge soon after the OCD's onset. While each person reacts differently, family members may exhibit one or more of the following.

Denial and minimization. Because OCD can be a frightening, strange, and bizarre disorder, an initial impulse is to pretend it is not there. This is called denial. Denial ranges from refusing to recognize that something is wrong to not acknowledging that something harmful is happening to the family. Another way of coping with OCD is to tell oneself that it is not so bad, doesn't have any effect on me, or to think it can be cured or eliminated in short order. This is called minimization. Thus, denial and minimization are often the first symptoms to appear. The denial and self-delusion are fueled by a mixture of love, fear, anger, and guilt. Denial and minimization can also occur in the professional community. As a result of denial, effective treatment may be delayed and that delay can be a form of denial.

Enabling. Because the atmosphere in a home with OCD is so often emotionally charged, everyone in the family tries to help. For all the right reasons, they do all the wrong things! They continue giving the person with OCD reassurance and comfort even when they know doing so is ineffective. Unfortunately, each compulsive effort at reassurance by the family is met with greater anxiety by the afflicted person. For example, an individual with OCD seeks comfort and support by "checking," but paradoxically the checking only increases the anxiety of the person with OCD.

High tolerance for inappropriate behavior. After chronic exposure to a living situation that can be illogical, arbitrary, and highly stressful, those around the individual with OCD might begin to believe that the illogical is logical and that the inappropriate is appropriate. What may once have seemed strange, unusual, or even bizarre can, over time, become accepted as commonplace, normal, and natural. Slowly, almost imperceptibly, family members can develop tolerance for the disorder—more and more accommodations are made as the afflicted's illness seems less and less strange. In time, the perceptions of those surrounding the person with OCD can become distorted.

Confusion and doubt. As the web of irrationality, perceptual distortion, and high tolerance of inappropriateness spreads, family members can become ensnared in their own web of doubt and uncertainty. They may experience difficulty maintaining healthy boundaries and take on the pain and hurt, as well as the confusion, of the person with OCD. Ambivalence about the person with OCD may become chronic: loved ones want to be closer to the person but also want to distance themselves to avoid further hurt. Many find it difficult to make decisions, because these decisions have often resulted in discomfort for the OCD-afflicted person. This, in turn, fuels anxiety in other family members. Loved ones often feel powerless and are, in fact, powerless in preventing compulsions or obsessions.

Hypervigilance. As the OCD exerts more and more influence over the family and loved ones, everyone can become more stressed and traumatized. This means everyone lives in more fear and becomes more sensitive to possible attack. They learn to scan for clues in order to feel safe. There may be little rest. Life has become too serious. Family members may have a difficult time letting go and being spontaneous. They have learned that danger lurks in spontaneity. Any situation has the potential to trigger an OCD episode and everyone is on alert status twenty-four hours a day, seven days a week. Consequently, family members have a steady supply of adrenaline in their blood. This, in turn, causes their heart to race, their pulse to accelerate, and their blood pressure to reach new heights. They are hyper-reactive to the least act which might evoke a traumatic response.

What Is the Second Set of Issues That Emerge as OCD Becomes More Entrenched in the Family System?

As OCD becomes more a part of the daily fabric and routine of the family, another set of issues begins to emerge. As loss and grief set in, the focus of the family changes and it becomes embroiled in these issues in an attempt to manage the unmanageable. They include some or all of the following.

Preoccupation with the OCD sufferer. Just as those with OCD are preoccupied with their obsessions and compulsions, family members frequently become preoccupied with the OCD. Many of their thoughts center around the person with the OCD. Increasingly, they may think of ways to manage the onslaught of obsessions and compulsions. They may participate in checking, answering the afflicted's unending questions, or trying to take control of the situation. There is a progressive focusing of attention on the OCD sufferer and a concurrent neglect of their own and other family members' feelings, wants, and needs. They, too, become obsessed.

Guilt. Family members often believe that they can't do quite enough. It seems as if they keep doing more things wrong than right. Despite their best intentions, the afflicted person continues to suffer. Trying to control the uncontrollable, loved ones can feel helpless, impotent, and frustrated, all of which can lead to a pervasive sense of failure and sadness. Since they are the well ones, they believe that they have little right to their feelings and no right to feel good. To make matters worse, the person with OCD may accuse family members of intentionally doing hurtful things. For example, family members may be accused of not being careful enough, considerate enough, or understanding enough. These accusations can generate tremendous self-doubt and guilt. Guilt-laden statements from the afflicted can assail the affected. For example, the sufferer might say something like,

"How could you do this to me?" Or, "You knew what would happen if you let me check again and you did."

Grief. As times goes on and the loved ones not only do not improve but actually get worse, many family members go through a protracted process of grieving, which is often neither diagnosed nor treated. The loss of a child, spouse, parent, or sibling to OCD can create a narrowing of attention and mourning no less severe than from an actual physical loss. In fact, sometimes the loss is more profound and enduring because it can last a lifetime.

Frozen feelings. Living in the intense, fear-driven atmosphere generated by OCD can lead those around the person to mute their feelings. Harsh judgments and direct reprimands can erode free expressions of feelings. Family members may feel empty, imprisoned, and caged-in as well as overwhelmed and fearful. Some feel grief and sadness in losing (or never getting a chance to develop) their relationship with the afflicted, but they are afraid to share these feelings because sharing the feelings may cause further pain for the person with OCD. Family members learn to separate from these painful feelings in order to cope. Recovery psychology teaches that separation from feelings fuels addiction. Addiction releases frozen feelings because the only time family members have access to their feelings is in the midst of addictive behavior. Thus, loved ones may be ripe for developing addictions and need to be screened for substance abuse and other addictions.

Indirect communication. Like other traumatized families, it may be difficult to talk about problems. Since feelings may not be expressed openly, communication can become indirect. One person may act as a messenger and go-between for others, or become "triangulated." When this happens, one family member will inquire about another not by asking that person, but by asking a third party because it seems safer. The result is confusion, frustration, anger, and hurt feelings.

Fatigue and exhaustion. Often, when the family is called upon to provide support, they are expected to become an endless emotional and financial resource, and at times even must monitor the life of the mentally ill sufferer. Many days are filled with the concerns, issues, and problems of the ill member. Worry, preoccupation, anxiety, and depression can leave affected family members drained personally and financially. This is compounded by the shame and secrecy surrounding this disorder. Family members tend to become isolated and do things by themselves, keeping the family secret hidden.

What Is the Third Set of Repercussions That the Family and Loved Ones Experience as OCD Progresses?

Just as with other serious and debilitating disorders, those under the influence of OCD begin to develop their own parallel disorder that can become chronic and progressive as well. At this phase of the family disorder, para-OCDism becomes more entrenched and family members or loved ones may exhibit some or all of the following symptoms.

Emotional symptoms. Just as OCD begins to affect the psychological well-being of the afflicted person, so too can intimates and loved ones be affected by the continual anxiety, doubt, and uncertainty. They can develop symptoms of post-traumatic stress disorder, including intrusive thoughts and feelings, a narrowing of their behaviors, and excessive excitability. They may also develop adjustment disorders, anxiety disorders, or depression, among other psychological problems.

Physical symptoms. As family members become stressed and fatigued, they can be at risk for a host of psychosomatic and stress-related illnesses. For example, migraines, colitis, or obesity can develop or be exacerbated. These are only a few of the physical health issues that can occur as the family attempts to cope with OCD.

Chronic low self-esteem. In this often traumatic atmosphere, it is easy to see how those surrounding the afflicted can feel "bad, sick, crazy, and dumb"[1] themselves. The shame and embarrassment of the person with OCD becomes contagious. Too often, family members narrow their social contacts. Isolation sets in as they become distanced from others. Because people with OCD can sometimes blame those closest to them, loved ones question their own self-worth and adequacy. Furthermore, because they are unable to protect the person with OCD from continued pain, they may feel overly and irrationally responsible.

All these ingredients become fertile breeding ground for the development of chronic low self-esteem.

Loss of self. Everyone in the family can suffer from progressive estrangement from the self. By living in continual reaction to the person with OCD, family members can suffer a gradual and progressive loss of self just like the person with OCD. Because they are frequently an ancillary part of treatment, they may feel invisible. Neglecting their own needs, they are at risk of becoming alienated from what they feel, think, want, or need. They can become a shell of their former self just like the person with OCD. Their spiritual life may suffer as they feel abandoned by God. Anger and blame toward God may be openly expressed in the family. Eventually, if untreated, some family members may experience a spiritual bankruptcy as profound as the person with OCD. Feelings have become replaced by an obsessive need to control, and a process of self-alienation culminates in a "loss of self."

How Will Knowledge of These Issues Help You?

I remember the glee in a client's eyes when he was told that he had a diagnosable and treatable neurophysiological disorder. Not only did he experience tremendous relief, but he was now able to proceed intelligently with treatment and recovery. Identification of OCD for the OCD sufferer is life-altering.

In a similar way, when the family and loved ones learn about OCD and identify their reactions to it, they can proceed with their own healing. When we label a problem, we can stop accepting the unacceptable. When we stop accepting the unacceptable, we open the door to our own healing. Without identification of the problems, it's difficult to know where to begin and what to work on. By identifying common factors, you begin to give these problems a name, create a useful vocabulary, and explore their nature. You can begin to see where you're stuck and where your foot is nailed to the floor.

You can begin to develop new ways of looking at the problems and learn to "relate to" the problem of OCD instead of "relate from" the OCD.[26] Learning this distinction can help you view your life and the life of the person with OCD in a more empowering light. Many of my clients have found the following metaphor helpful in learning this distinction. One of my clients called it the "Circle-In, Circle-Out" distinction.

Imagine a circle. When you are totally in one of your issues, so much so that you don't even realize it, you metaphorically have both feet inside the circle. In pre-recovery you will enable or participate in your loved one's compulsions or rituals and have no idea that you are doing both yourself and the OCD sufferer a disservice or actually prolonging the illness. The person with OCD loses and you lose. This is what happens when both feet are inside the circle.

If you have one foot outside the circle of your issue and one foot inside the circle of your issue, then you are aware that you are in your issue, but you can't get out of it—at least at that time. You remain stuck and keep doing the same negative behavior over and over again, but at least you know you are doing it. You know, for example, that if you answer your loved one's questions, or help him or her check the stove, you are enabling. But you will still participate because you fear your loved one's anger or, incorrectly, believe you will ease the afflicted's discomfort.

When you have both feet outside the circle, however, you are no longer relating *from* but *to* your issue. It no longer runs you. Rather, when you are relating to your issue, it's as if you can hold it at arm's length and be more dispassionate. You are somewhat unattached and more objective. In the above example, you not only know that to participate in your loved one's compulsions is harmful, but you are able to keep your issue in check and not participate in enabling behavior, even though your lack of participation may create a disturbance. Your mind tells you one thing and, this time, your body and nervous system are in alignment. I bet each of you have been faced with many situations just like this.

When Are These Issues Most Likely to Surface?

These common issues are most likely to surface or increase during times of stress. Transition points are also highly stressful. These points could include unwelcome events such as the loss of a job, or change in occupation, or unusual job stress, illness, or death. Ironically, joyful events can also be stressful, such as marriages, births, birthdays, visits from relatives, holidays, and even vacations. When the family's routine is disrupted in any way, issues may become more apparent. Any of these transition points can exacerbate the core coping tendencies we have discussed. Since these events and transition points are a part of everybody's life, you can be sure another one is just around the corner for all of us. Just as OCD is stress-sensitive and obsessions and compulsions tend to increase with stress, the reactive feelings and behaviors of the family tend to increase also. You can, however, learn to more effectively handle these periods so that your family life will be smoother and you can stay off the roller coaster more and more.

How Do You Take Care of Yourself When Confronting Your Core Issues?

You take care of yourself with time, with attention, and with tenderness.

I encourage you to be patient with yourself as you learn about these issues and how you can begin to work on them. Lasting change takes time and patience. Changing deeply-rooted patterns of thoughts, feelings, and behavior requires time and effort.

With a better understanding of what you're up against, you may notice an immediate sense of relief. You may also experience increased pain as you grasp more fully the enormity and complexity of the task ahead. In addition to giving the changes time to take place, you will want to give yourself additional time—to rest, and to take care of yourself.

Patience could include recognizing that change may feel like two steps forward and one step back. You may find yourself feeling discouraged and thinking, "Oh my gosh. I thought I had handled that issue, and yet here it is again." Patience might also include watching the person with OCD during an OCD episode and having the insight to know that, as bad as it is now, it will pass.

Healing yourself and your family will require your attention. You need to give your attention to the matter of getting well. You will not need to focus on recovery every minute, but it will require your focus. There is a saying that "energy flows where attention goes." While excessive focus on the negative impact of OCD could be exhausting, attentive focus on what you can do will help you move along in your healing.

Lastly, this journey will require much love and tenderness for yourself. You are embarking on a wonderful voyage of discovery and you will be learning many new skills. Just as you would be tender with your child as he or she learns something new and difficult, you will want to give yourself the same loving care and support.

It's important to remember that movement forward is getting up one more time than you fall down. That is the true measure of success. Don't expect perfection from yourself. Time, attention, and tenderness are the bywords of this stage.

What Are the Major Stumbling Blocks During This Period?

During the time you're confronting your own core issues that result from the wake of OCD, the biggest stumbling block is underestimating the tenacity of these issues while overestimating your ability to handle them. For example, rather than feeling overwhelmed by them, you might think, "Oh, this will be easy work. Now that I know that being preoccupied with the person with OCD or enabling the person's behavior isn't good for either me or the person with OCD, I'll stop doing that." You will quickly discover that this is easier said than done.

These patterns that have often been with you for a long time are insidious and may have begun to feel "natural." It has been said that it takes twenty-one days to change a habit. Well, you probably have many habits and deeply embedded patterns to change, so it's important to remember this. Failing to keep this in mind can lead to discouragement. Remember, when you fall face down, you will at least be moving forward!

Other stumbling blocks during this stage include not having a recovery plan, not getting appropriate treatment, not having adequate knowledge and support, and not taking care of your mind, body, and spirit.

This is the stage in which you have a choice: you can either use these words as another way to indict yourself or others, or these words can become a vocabulary that can act as a springboard to the next stage of your development.

Can These Issues Apply to Others Who Do Not Come From a Family Under the Influence of OCD?

Absolutely. I have mentioned several times the similarity between the atmosphere and issues in a family with OCD and in those of families dealing with other chronic illnesses. The effects of all traumas are remarkably similar.[60] It matters little what they are. Whether the trauma is human in origin, such as physical, sexual, or emotional abuse, or natural in origin, like fires and earthquakes, there is a shattering of the self. Regardless of whether people are suffering from the influence of OCD, schizophrenia, cancer, lupus, MS, Alzheimer's, or a host of other possible plights, they experience a recognizable cluster of problems and may see themselves as helpless, bad, and living in a meaningless world.

That said, however, living with a person with OCD has its own unique stamp. You're dealing with a neurological or brain disorder that waxes and wanes. As mentioned in Chapter One, about 15 percent of people with OCD show progressive deterioration in job and social functioning. About 5 percent have an intermittent course with minimal or no symptoms between episodes. The remainder of people with OCD experience the coming and going of symptoms, with seemingly little predictability.[1] This means living with OCD is like riding a roller coaster without the happy excitement that accompanies it. The sufferer might be relatively symptom free for days, weeks, even months, when suddenly the OCD strikes again.

Will You Be Able to Get Rid of These Problems?

If you think of "these problems" as OCD, the answer is "No, you won't be able to get rid of the OCD." If the question is, "Will I be able to get rid of, or minimize, the effects of these common issues that occur in people and families with OCD?" the answer is "Yes." You can grow and make significant progress in your reactions to living with and loving someone who has OCD. In fact, better questions include the following: "How can I use these problems to further my own growth and intentions?" "How can I continue to grow and thrive as a person in spite of the OCD?" or even "How can I view the presence of OCD in my loved one as a challenge to be surmounted rather than a curse to be endured?"

Another way to look at this stage in your healing is called "conscious incompetence." Not unlike the stages or course of the hero's journey, which I'll describe in the chapters "Healing Yourself" and "Healing the Family," these healing stages comprise four steps.

Steps one and two are "unconscious incompetence" and "conscious incompetence." In "unconscious incompetence," you don't even know enough to know something is wrong. This closely resembles how you probably were feeling when you didn't know that OCD was the problem or what to do about it. When you examine your problems and begin to deal with your personal issues, at least you realize that something is wrong and you have something to do with it. Now you're dealing with the problems in a state of "conscious incompetence." This is the beginning of liberation and healing. From this place you can begin to change in ways that are powerfully helpful for you and for the person with OCD.

When you realize that many of the problems you and your family experience are a result of OCD and that there are things you can do to improve the situation, you have one foot out of the circle. You are aware of the issue although you may not always be able to do something about it or stop your destructive behavior. You are "consciously incompetent." This is a much more powerful place to move from than may first appear.

The last two steps, "conscious competence" and "unconscious competence" go along with the later stages of healing. You'll hear more about these in the chapters "Moving Beyond," "Getting It Together," and "Healing the Family."

With these new distinctions that you are learning in this chapter, you are on your way to recovering from the effects of OCD on your family. There is much to be hopeful about. Most families are able to recognize their core issues by becoming more aware of the impact of OCD on them, and once they do, they move to the next stage where positive and constructive things can be done about these problems, beyond merely naming them.

—w—

CHAPTER 5

Moving Beyond—
Shifting Perspectives

—∞—

What is "Moving Beyond"?

Moving beyond occurs when your focus shifts from a preoccupation with OCD and the OCD sufferer to other arenas of life that require your time, attention, and effort. The OCD has been diagnosed. You know you have been under its influence and have developed certain issues *of your own* that may need healing. You now also discover that there is life beyond OCD. You are no longer constantly ensnared by it; OCD has been put into proportion and scaled down to its appropriate importance in your life. It no longer occupies all or even the central portion of your existence. As a result, you are able to develop a life alongside of, and in addition to, OCD.

Because you are able to respond to a wide variety of life's offerings instead of just one of its problems, you are now ready to confront your own issues in life. You matter! You have the right to an existence independently from OCD. Many people under the influence of OCD never reach this stage of healing. So, congratulations! You deserve acknowledgment for your stamina and resilience. You have moved beyond the influence of OCD. It doesn't matter for how long or short a period of time. You have moved out from under the influence of OCD, and you have moved beyond OCD in that moment. The more you create these moments of moving beyond, the stronger the emotional muscles you use for recovery become.

What Does the World of Moving Beyond Look Like?

You actually experience a perceptual shift. Things look different. They sound different and feel different. Your mind is less clouded. You have a new outlook with which to create the meaning of your life. You are moving beyond the trauma and the drama. In Rabbi Harold Kushner's moving book, *When Bad Things Happen to Good People*, he suggests that the bad things that happen to us and our loved ones do not have any meaning when they first happen.[38] We redeem these losses by giving them meaning. Only later, when we remove ourselves from their influence, can we move beyond such disempowering and dispiriting questions as, "Why did this happen to me or my loved one?" or "What did I (or they) do wrong?" to more meaningful and productive questions like, "What do I do now that this has happened to me (us)?" Questions like the former center upon the past, where blame, doubt, and confusion reign, while questions like the latter open the door to the future. Questions like the former reinforce our suffering, while questions like the latter lead us to a more positive place.

A telling example can be found in Martin Gray's book, *For Those I Loved*. A survivor of the Holocaust, Gray became successful after his trauma. He married a woman he loved and raised a family. But one day Gray again lost his whole family when his wife and children were killed in a forest fire. In his book he tells how, once again, he rebuilt his life by focusing on the future. Although tempted to demand an inquiry into what caused the fire, he committed his life to preventing future fires. He explained that any attempt to investigate would only lead him against others (for example, "Whose fault was this?"). He believed life must be lived *for* something, not just *against* something.

The sages, the mystics, the healers, and even modern researchers all agree that happiness and success in life are relatively independent of our circumstances. In *The Pursuit of Happiness,* author and scholar David Myers[44] documents the vast literature that shows that outside circumstances have little to do with happiness. What matters in the pursuit of happiness and well-being is *attitude.* The personal meaning one ascribes to life's circumstances and events are critical. This does not mean that you look for or create suffering, although extracting meaning from suffering ennobles and heals. Victor Frankel, the psychiatrist who lived through the horrors of the Holocaust, wrote, "The striving to find meaning in one's life is the primary motivational force in man." Breaking out of the endless suffering of OCD's wake can have little to do with any of the objective circumstances in your life. Once you get beyond your circumstances, you are in the process of healing.

What Are the Major Signs of Moving Beyond OCD?

First and foremost, you know you are in this stage of healing when you begin to feel better. Roy C.[6] says, "A good method is to treat yourself at least as well as the person you care about." Whether or not anyone else has changed, you have! You are no longer constantly consumed by the weight of OCD. You feel an enormous heaviness lifted from your shoulders. Your muscle tension decreases every moment that you are beyond the grasp of OCD. You can breathe more easily and freely. For the most part, you are off "red alert."

But as you begin to feel better, a curious phenomenon often happens. You feel guilty, but guilty in distinctly different ways than before. In the early stages of recovery you felt guilty for not "helping" or for not participating in the compulsions of the person with OCD. You could also have felt guilty for not being more understanding, more patient, or more kind.

Now, however, you're feeling guilty for breaking away from the OCD, for having an independent life, even a happy life, with real moments of pleasure, even while the person with OCD is still suffering. Since it is largely irrational, the guilt can be momentary. As soon as you recognize it, you have the opportunity to challenge it and assert your own needs and rights. *You must do this!* Even though you have moments of guilt, you continue to go out more and take better care of yourself and others.

What Kinds of Shifts May Take Place in This Stage of Healing?

Another shift or sign of moving beyond OCD is that you begin to feel better in a variety of ways, not just emotionally. Your physical health and sense of well-being improve. You have more interest in almost everything. You have more energy, you sleep better, and many of the physical complaints we talked about earlier lessen or disappear. Your spirit is back and you are genuinely looking forward to the future—because you see positive things ahead.

You may also notice that you begin responding with love and compassion in situations in which you were once angry and judgmental. When you are angry in this stage—which you certainly will be at times—you bounce back quickly, because you have learned to deal with the anger in effective ways. You are now involved in what author Thomas Moore[43] calls "the care of the soul."

To go beyond the influence of OCD will necessitate boundaries—setting them and keeping them. Limits are needed in order to have your own life. When you are moving beyond, you might find that you do not answer the OCD sufferer's questions or participate knowingly in their rituals. You no longer feel bad about these kinds of decisions. In fact, it is healthy—for you and for the person with OCD. If you can't get over the guilt and it continues to interfere with your taking care of yourself, you might want to seek professional help and consult a doctor, a therapist, or a member of the clergy.

How Can You Move Beyond the Influence of OCD?

It is important to note that it is impossible to be in a caring relationship with someone with OCD and *never* fall prey to the influence of OCD. In order to move beyond this influence, you need a method to break the spell when it has you in its grip. When you think of the family and loved ones as being under the influence of OCD, or under a kind of spell, you become open to the possibilities in the rich fields of clinical hypnosis and altered states of consciousness. These offer powerful methods to further take control of your life.

One of the most important and learnable skills from these fields is "trance busting." Trance busting[26] is any intervention that frees you from the trance you are in. After freeing yourself, you can connect with other, more powerful states of mind. Busting a trance can be as simple as shifting your body, a strategy that is remarkably powerful for brief trances. Sometimes, when the trance is deep and profound, the only way to bust it is to undergo psychotherapy.

Trance busting can occur in a number of ways. One trance-busting method is to disrupt or break up the trance; another is to name the trance. Both are based on the psychological principle called "prepotent responses," which states that a more powerful response will interrupt a less powerful one.

We experience a variety of negative trances; some relate to OCD and some don't. For example, I once decided to go on a body cleanse. I stopped eating solid foods and began nutritional supplements. Whenever I'd take my supplements, I would narrow my focus, shrink my attention, and suggest to myself that this situation (my food deprivation) was terrible and unfair. I would then feel bad. The result was a predictable downward spiral in which I felt more and more victimized and helpless. By the third week of "deprivation" and "food trauma," I was under the influence of a mild to moderate "poor me" trance. My attitude reflected this "poor me" trance.

When I labeled this state of mind as a type of hypnotic spell, I could use my knowledge about disrupting or busting trances to free myself. Hypnosis teaches us that if we aren't in one trance, we will be in another. Trance states are very common. We can choose the state of mind under whose influence we want to be. Can you remember a time, for example, when you were feeling absolutely horrible? And then somebody very important telephoned and you immediately switched states from an "everything's horrible" trance to an "everything's fine" trance.

One of my friends, a chiropractor, woke up one day and found that he couldn't lift his right hand above his shoulder. One surgery and fifteen months later, he still couldn't get his hand over his shoulder, and now he is on work disability. Another friend started auto-dialysis because he has a life-threatening kidney disease. Four times each and every day, whether sick or tired, he must spend an hour "exchanging" his blood with the vital fluid in a hermetically sealed container by way of plumbing tubes surgically inserted into his body. He, of course, isn't able to do very much. Going to a movie is a major logistics problem. How's that for trouble?

I decided to start busting my "poor me" trance with a little help from my friends. Whenever I felt myself falling into a "poor me" trance, I imagined my two friends. It was impossible to hold my negative trance and an image of them simultaneously. I can pop myself out of most negative trances by interrupting them with a more powerful or prepotent image. In order to break your trance regarding OCD, you might remember that there really are many people worse off than you. I'm sure you can think of at least one person. If you can't, volunteer to spend an afternoon at a burn center.

UCLA psychiatrist Jeffrey Schwartz' familiar refrain, "It's not me—it's my OCD"[52] is an example of trance busting by naming OCD. This trance buster correctly (and positively) attributes the problem to a neurophysiological condition rather than to the core self. Positive trance states seem to expand your options when named, while negative trance states seem to cause you to lose power. When you can view OCD as a trance, or describe it, then you are bigger than the trance and it releases its hold on you. When you name OCD, then you (*either* the person with OCD *or* the family) are also bigger than the OCD and it releases its hold on you.

What Other Strategies Can You Use to Help Yourself?

Master hypnotists use hypnotic principles and phenomena in healing.[17] Becoming familiar with these principles can also help you heal. As you read through the following examples, the deeper and wiser parts of you can use these examples so that when new situations arise, you can recall and/or extrapolate from them. Be aware of how you can apply them to your own unique situation.

The hypnotic phenomenon of age progression,[26] where the person progresses or "goes into the future" to solve a problem, is a common hypnotic strategy. For example, I worked with a man whose fiancée was a woman with a severe hand-washing compulsion. During one of his therapy sessions, he encountered a part of himself he called "Recovery Man." In his imagination, Recovery Man is free of the tyranny of OCD's wake and is the man my client wants to be when he is with his girlfriend. Recovery Man understands OCD and its impact on loved ones.

Recovery Man became my co-therapist as well my client. Whenever he was in a difficult situation, needed advice, or was at a critical juncture in his relationship with his fiancée, he would "consult" Recovery Man. Since Recovery Man knew more than either of us, both of us were often amazed at the insight and foresight of this part of his psyche. Recovery Man was especially skillful at identifying enabling behaviors and could intervene to stop him from checking and doing those things for his fiancée that she could do for herself.

Another client learned to access and develop a part of her psyche she called "Future Woman." Like Recovery Man, the Future Woman part of her is older, wiser, and more mature than she. Unlike Recovery Man, however, Future Woman is from a different time and a different galaxy. She was sent from another dimension to guide and counsel my client, who was under the deep spell of her son's OCD. As she progressed in her work, Future Woman began to evolve. My client discovered that it was only Future Woman's perspective that relieved the tremendous acute pain she felt when she thought of her boy's OCD.

"Anchoring" is another powerful tool that you can use to deal with the impact of OCD.[26] It is the tendency for any one element of an experience to bring forth the entire experience. For example, certain scents, like the smell of chocolate-chip cookies baking in the oven or oak burning and crackling in the fireplace, can "trance-port" you to another time and place and bring back the thoughts and feelings associated with that memory. Couples often have a song that they call "their song." Whenever they hear it (including long after they are together!), both are immediately reminded of their feelings for each other.

"Anchors" trigger experiences that can range from joyful to debilitating. These experiences are rich sources of abilities and capacities. The sight of a sunset, the sound of the ocean's waves, or the warmth of a fire can elicit comfort and security, unless each memory was the occasion of a traumatic event. One client, for example, was told of his child's OCD in front of a fireplace. Now, whenever he sees a fireplace, he breaks out in a cold sweat. For a long time, all he knew was that he couldn't be around fireplaces.

Another client would get irritable whenever she heard the sound of ice cubes falling in a glass. Both the adult child of two alcoholic parents and the mother of a beautiful three-year girl with severe OCD, she never forgot the turmoil that would follow cocktail hour when she was a little girl.

Every sensory experience (visual, auditory, kinesthetic, olfactory, and gustatory), can serve as a potential anchor for the experience at hand. Seeing the flashing red light of a police car in my rear view mirror still elicits an exaggerated startle response. Hearing the "Star Spangled Banner" still evokes a sense of love for my country. The sight of a cross or a Star of David or the American flag, for example, are all visual anchors that produce rich associations. Hearing the sound of a car backfiring is a strong negative anchor for many Vietnam veterans. Certain postures and movements can serve as anchors for various states of awareness. If you were to put your thumb in your mouth, you might access a familiar state of consciousness, one you experienced as a small child when you sucked your thumb and felt comforted.

Anchors occur naturally or they can be "installed." They can be formed intentionally or unintentionally by a parent, a therapist, or by you. Mark is a good example. He didn't want to see his son suffer, so he would help him count the number of times he saw the color red in the last hour before bedtime. Before his son could go to sleep, he had to end up with a certain number or combination of a favored number. When Mark wasn't in recovery, this meant helping his son count to "protect" him. As Mark came to understand the destructiveness of this counting, he decided to create a reminder, or anchor, to prevent his behavior. Every time he experienced his desire to protect his son in an unhealthy manner, he would stroke his upper chest. After awhile, just stroking the top of his chest reminded him of his desire to protect his son in a healthy way. He'd "fire" this anchor whenever he was tempted to enable his son's OCD.

In the chapter on core issues, you discovered how easy it is to split off from yourself and from uncomfortable situations. You can be dissociated from your body. You can be dissociated from your feelings. You can be dissociated from your resources, too. Dissociation, however, is also a natural and spontaneous process occurring in everyone because it has protective and life-enhancing functions. When a person is in charge of a dissociation's "on" and "off" button, he or she has a powerful tool for dealing with any kind of experience or activity from a comfortable distance. When you are in reverie or daydreaming, for example, you are in a slightly dissociated state of consciousness and, in its most positive and creative sense, you can fantasize from a comfortable distance. John used dissociation to disconnect from the suffering he would experience when he'd worry about his parents, both of whom had OCD.

What the mind perceives is relative and arbitrary.[17] Your assessments of "reality" are at least as much determined by what you *think and feel* as by the circumstances in which you find yourself. As your beliefs interact with an event, you co-create the meaning of the event. Consequently, there is the opportunity to participate in the very creation of "reality." There is the possibility to increasingly take charge of your experiences.

Each of these tools helps you take charge of your state of consciousness—or your trance states. Taking charge of your trance states is an assertion of responsibility and an act of heroism. When you take charge of your trance states, you accept without judgment and condemnation any information the external world presents. You are comfortable with multiple realities. You do not attach or identify with any given one.[26]

How Do You Know You Are Dealing Effectively With OCD?

All of the above signs of moving beyond and getting better are indicators that you're dealing more effectively with OCD. Another measure of your increasing effectiveness in dealing with OCD is a major shift in your beliefs, feelings, behaviors, and eventually attitudes. As you progress in your recovery, you will see one or more of the following shifts:

- the shift from few or no boundaries to healthy limit setting— for example, no checking.

- the shift from seeing the glass of your life as half empty to seeing it as half full—for example, you can see some of the positive things the person with OCD is doing, not just the negative.

- the shift from a sense of doing more things wrong than right to doing more things right than wrong—for example, believing that on most days you can live with the influence of OCD.

- the shift from enabling behavior to a kind of "tough love," "compassionate listening," "reality discipline," or as Al-Anon puts it, "detaching with love"—for example, saying no to participating in a loved one's ritual.

- the shift from reacting to OCD in automatic, unconscious, knee-jerk ways to pausing and consciously choosing your response in a way that's healthy for you and the person with OCD—for example, you get hooked less and less by the OCD or the person with OCD.

- the shift from doing the same things again and again and expecting different results to trying new behaviors—for example, creating a new family tradition instead of complying with a compulsion.

All of these shifts are indications that you are recognizing, addressing, and dealing with the core issues we talked about in the last chapter and moving beyond them. You're on the mythic hero's journey. Success means getting it right more times than getting it wrong. It is not about getting it right all the time. Success is a commitment to making your growth a priority and using OCD as fuel for the journey. It might involve using the mythological perspective to see OCD as a sacred wound requiring a heroic quest and a determination to heal the kingdom.

Jim, who we met earlier, had to continually remind himself it was the OCD, not Mary, that created so much suffering. He had to remind himself that he had a life, too, and that there were only so many things he could do and many things he couldn't do. He repeated daily what has become known as the "Serenity Prayer": "God grant me the serenity to accept the things I cannot change, the courage to change the things I can, and the wisdom to know the difference."

Is It Necessary to Deal With Your Past to Go Beyond?

In general, it's much more productive to deal with present concerns and future possibilities. The Newtonian world with its linear model of cause and effect shows that the past determines the present, whereas the newer cybernetic, quantum model shows that one's vision of the future greatly affects the present.

Dr. Charles Garfield,[20] a pioneer in peak performance and personal success, found that peak performers in all disciplines are alike in that they ask, "What will this situation look like when it is working perfectly?" He goes on to say that other questions "build bridges from the future back to the present....The peak performer uses *feedforward* to learn from the projected future." In addition, peak performers are able to sustain their efforts and commit themselves to compelling missions that extend beyond their own personal reach.

There are times, however, when it might be wise to deal with the past. One of the indicators of the need to deal with the past is when you keep putting your earlier life experiences and expectations into your present circumstances. By this I mean that you allow how you thought, felt, and behaved earlier in your life to determine how you think, feel, and act today. You keep yourself stuck as a result, because you are reacting (not responding) to some present circumstance because of past experience. The rational (often out of consciousness) goes: "Because I handled a situation similar to this before, I'll use the same strategy now." Unfortunately, this is like driving your car by looking in the rearview mirror. You see what you have passed or where you've been, but you are missing what is ahead or where you're going. This is neither a good driving strategy nor a good life strategy.

If you find yourself doing things that don't seem to be getting you anywhere, and in fact are causing you a lot of discomfort, you may find dealing with your past and its impact on your present valuable. At times, old patterns from the past may blind you. If you're doing the same thing again and again and it keeps turning out wrong, get suspicious. When you're aware that this is happening, it's time to think of new and different ways of being and doing. Talk to someone you trust and get another view. You may want to seek professional help. For example, join a therapy or support group and/or get individual and family counseling. When you can separate the past from the present, you can begin to create a better life for yourself.

Some people are afraid that if they explore the past, they will get lost there. This is an unfortunate misconception. From my experience, working with thousands of people, exploring the past can be an opportunity to create a new and more conscious life today.

What Can You Do With All This Information?

Let it settle, let it simmer, and be curious. Being inquisitive is the most helpful attitude to have toward the knowledge you're learning. Ask yourself what is going on between you and your family, look to see where your foot is nailed to the floor, and be in an active inquiry about where you're struggling.

Here is a caveat, though. Be careful about being overly zealous with your new knowledge, particularly with the person with OCD. It's more important, for example, to demonstrate your knowledge in the form of compassion than to just talk about it. The goal of your healing is to "walk your walk," not "talk your walk." Your actions will speak louder than your words.

Am I Suggesting That You Stop Being Kind, Caring, or Giving?

Not at all. Kindness and compassion fuel everyone's healing in the family. You should, however, stop the enabling. Not only does enabling deprive the person with OCD of the opportunity to learn and grow, it actually fuels the illness so that it can manifest and grow. In the words of Roy C., "It feeds the disease like bellows fan a fire." So, while you will need to stop doing things that aren't helpful, continue doing all the things you like to do that are loving. If you enjoy buying the person flowers, continue. If you like taking the person to the movies, go. If you like sending a note, keep that up. But if you're participating in the OCD, stop.

How Will You Know If You Are Enabling?

If you are doing something for the person that he or she is capable of doing, you are enabling, unless, of course, the person is too young or too ill to do it himself or herself. While reassurance can provide short-term tension reduction for people with OCD, one way to know that you're participating in the OCD is when what you say and do increases the level of anxiety and tension that the person with OCD experiences. Watching the results of your actions on the person with OCD is a good way to evaluate whether you're helping or hurting the recovery process for all of you.

If you find you can't stop doing those things, see a professional and get some coaching. Seeing a professional might be the very move that leads you beyond your core issues. A good therapist is like a good coach, helping you spot weaknesses and strengths in your game and encouraging you in your progress. Working with a professional may be the only way you can create an effective distance from the hypnotic and spell-binding influence of OCD.

How Do You Stop Doing What Seems So Natural and Loving?

Let your new knowledge lead the way and let it form the basis of your commitments, especially to yourself. You now have more information and wisdom about how to deal with your own particular issues. Your heart has both the tendency to provide relief for the other person, as well as provide relief for you. However, using your heart first with OCD can be a flawed strategy. OCD requires that you use your head first. Save your heart to express your love. Decide on what your new strategies and commitments are and let these determine your decisions.

How Important Are Friends or a Social Life to Moving Beyond?

Relationships are the soil where personal growth occurs. Therefore, it's important not only to keep up your friendships and social life, but actually pursue them vigorously both within and without the OCD community. There is an old saying, "We're only as sick as our secrets." Having someone with whom you can share all your thoughts and feelings is healing. This is a journey that's best taken with the support of others. You'll know if it's the right person. You will feel better because you have spoken meaningfully to another and shared how you feel. If you don't feel better, or if you feel shut down, criticized, controlled, stupid, or bad, pick someone else. When you feel any of these feelings, that's a sign that this person is probably not the right one to hear what you need to say.

Use a strategy[27] called "share-check-share." Share a little about yourself and your situation. Check or watch how the person responds to you. Based on what you get back, decide whether you're safe to share more or whether it would be better to pull back. This can be a useful technique, especially if your tendency is all or none, which means you're either being guarded and secretive or telling everything when you first meet a person.

Besides the aspect of sharing, just getting out with friends and away from the situation at home can be refreshing. Getting away can be as simple as taking a walk, having lunch with a friend, going to a movie, or even spending a few days away by yourself. These simple activities can have a profound effect on you. As a result of these practices, you have more room, or spaciousness, for life's inevitable pain and loss.

How Can You Deal With Your Need to Fix or Control OCD?

At one time, you may have been controlling by not allowing the person with OCD to be responsible for his or her own disorder. You made decisions for the sufferer that he or she could have made. It's natural to take over and compensate for someone who is ill or otherwise incapacitated.

At this point, you need to be the judge of whether or not you're controlling. Remember that very little in life is all or nothing, and you need to move away from a black and white stance to heal.[26] Probably, there are times when you are too controlling—when you're trying to control the course and the progression of the illness, for example. As we've seen, that is impossible to do. Trying to do the impossible can be "crazy-making." Just when you "think" you've got things under control, everything unravels and you're back on the roller coaster. You cannot control OCD, and you need to give up all illusions of controlling it. You might just as well try to control the weather or assume responsibility for a sunny day.

There are other times, though, when you are not in control and you need to be. That is when you're reacting in an automatic knee-jerk fashion instead of consciously choosing your responses. Developing and practicing new responses will require self-control and behaviors based on your new knowledge and commitments. Once again, remember that your goal is to strengthen new muscles. You will experience more freedom when you see your full range of choices and assume appropriate responsibility.

Thinking in terms of opposites, like black and white, often people perceive that control is either good or bad. It is neither. Rather, it depends on the situation and what is driving the control. If OCD is driving the control, nothing productive will happen and your efforts will be futile. But when your vision and commitment are driving the control, then you're creating a healing atmosphere for yourself and everybody in your life.

For example, if you are waiting to go to the Little League game and your wife is still washing her hands, you have a choice. Each choice you make illustrates a different way of exercising or not exercising control. One option is to get increasingly angry and to attempt to badger or shame her into stopping her rituals. This is an example of trying to control the illness. Not exercising personal control when it is needed, on the other hand, would be allowing yourself to react in unhelpful and damaging ways like yelling, begging, or pleading with the person to refrain from the ritual. This is an example of attempting to control the other person and abdicating self-control instead of controlling your own anger and frustration. Letting yourself explode might temporarily release some of your anger and frustration, but, in the long run, it certainly won't help you, your family, or the person with OCD.

A better option would be to have a decision-making plan already in effect. An example of such a plan would be, "Everybody waits only five minutes before they leave, even if Mom is crying." Thus, an already-established plan—one in which Mom was informed ahead of time that everyone would leave after five minutes—determines what is to be done, not the immediate, particular situation. Self-control is called for in either situation and beginning to exercise that control creates a healing atmosphere for yourself and everyone else.

In *Getting Control: Overcoming Your Obsessions and Compulsions,* OCD specialist Dr. Lee Baer encourages his readers to carry four statements on a card. While they were directed toward overcoming obsessions and compulsions, they apply to all of us who are learning new ways to exercise healthy control.

1. You cannot always control your thoughts.

2. You cannot control your feelings.

3. But you *can* always control your behavior.

4. As you change your behavior, your thoughts and feelings will also change.

This is learning to control in the best sense of the word: self-control. Remember, you cannot control your feelings. They rise and fall like the tides in the ocean, but you can control your actions.

How Do You Confront the OCD Sufferer?

Your job is not to confront those with OCD. Your job is to continue loving them and supporting them, not in their obsessions or rituals, but with your faith in their ability to get well. Communicate with confidence your belief that they can have an active role in their own healing and can improve their situation.

What Can You Expect From the Person With OCD?

When you're moving beyond your issues, don't expect to be thanked, especially if the person with OCD is not in a daily, ongoing program of healing. Initially, the person with OCD may be angry and confused that you're not helping in the usual ways. That's a big part of the problem with enabling: OCD sufferers rely on loved ones in the very ways that rob them of their power to grow and change. They cannot learn, for example, that they don't have to clean every spot or count every space in order to be safe when you give in to their rituals. While they may not thank you at the moment for not enabling their OCD, if they are working on their own recovery and healing, they will thank you—perhaps an hour later, a day later, or whenever they realize that by not enabling them you're really supporting them in their recovery and healing.

The goal in this recovery journey is for both the person with OCD and the family to function as well as they can. It works like a dance. One person leads the way and the other follows. And, at times, the lead switches.

Are You Selfish and Thinking Only of Yourself If You Move On?

If the person with OCD is well into recovery and keeps telling you that you're selfish, it might pay to listen and ask yourself about your activities and intentions. However, if your loved one with OCD is just beginning in recovery or refuses to participate in a healing process, more than likely he or she *will* tell you that you're being selfish and thinking only of yourself. This might be a good opportunity to pause and think about the difference between "selfishness" and "self-caring." Do not accept this feedback at face value. Get input from an objective third party, preferably someone who knows your situation. It could be a close friend. Sometimes a professional therapist who understands OCD and its impact on the family can make all the difference in your healing.

You have undoubtedly been used to taking care of someone else, placating, adjusting, and believing that you can change unchangeable things or make things better for the person with OCD. The OCD sufferer may accuse you of being selfish or self-centered when you are no longer devoting all your attention to him or her, or giving attention in the same way you used to. Change is threatening even when it is necessary and healthy.

Since you are probably not used to caring for yourself, you naturally may feel uncomfortable and worry that the person with OCD is right and you really are "selfish." Remember that you are not abandoning the person with OCD by focusing on yourself. Ultimately, focusing on yourself and your needs helps you and your loved one.

Do You Have Specific Rights as a Family Member of Someone With OCD?

Moving beyond develops from a belief system that legitimizes self-acceptance. When para-OCDs claim their rights as sufferers too, they confront their central therapeutic issue: taking care of themselves. Having moved beyond victimization, they accept the responsibility for becoming the person they want to be. They become architects of a new life.

Your rights are the same as those of every other human being. Visualize the person you most admire standing in front of you. Now tell this person what his or her rights are. List them. Now consider the idea that these same rights and these same human privileges are yours, too.

In one of my first adult children of alcoholics' psychotherapy groups, a woman named Sue developed her own "bill of rights"[27] and brought it to share with others in her group. Like survivors of all traumas, her bill of rights is so universal that it speaks to para-OCDs as well, and I have modified them accordingly.

1. You have a right to all those good times that you have longed for.

2. You have a right to joy in this life, right here, right now—not just a momentary rush of euphoria but something more substantive.

3. You have a right to relax and have fun.

4. You have a right to actively pursue people, places, and situations that will help you in achieving a good life.

5. You have a right to say "no" whenever you believe or feel something is not safe or you are not ready.

6. You have a right to not participate in either the active or passive "crazy-making" behavior of spouses, parents, siblings, and others.

7. You have a right to take calculated risks and to experiment with new strategies.

8. You have a right to change your tune, your strategy, and your funny equations.

9. You have a right to mess up, make mistakes, blow it, disappoint yourself, and fall short of the mark.

10. You have a right to leave the company of people who deliberately or inadvertently put you down, lay a guilt trip on you, and manipulate or humiliate you, including the person with OCD or any other member of your family.

11. You have a right to all of your feelings.

12. You have a right to trust your feelings, your judgment, your hunches, and your intuition.

13. You have a right to develop yourself as a whole person emotionally, spiritually, mentally, physically, and psychologically.

14. You have a right to express all of your feelings in a nondestructive way and at a safe time and place.

15. You have a right to as much time as you need to initiate change with this new information and these new ideas.

16. You have a right to sort out the bill of goods that the OCD sold you—to take the acceptable and dump the unacceptable.

17. You have a right to a mentally healthy, sane way of existence, though it will deviate in part, or all, from another's philosophy of life.

18. You have a right to carve out your place in this world.

19. You have a right to follow any of the above rights, to live your life the way you want to, and not wait until the person with OCD gets well, gets happy, seeks help, or admits there is a problem.

What Are the Major Pitfalls During This Stage?

There are several pitfalls to watch out for during this period of your healing. One is a lack of endurance. In your enthusiasm and desire to move ahead, it may be easier to sprint for awhile, and then give up when it doesn't work as quickly or as well as the way you had hoped. It's critically important to endure. Hanging in there and getting up one more time than you fall down are critical. OCD is resilient, so you must be more resilient. This is not the time or place for black and white thinking, such as believing that you're either making all the right changes or you're not. You're probably making some right ones and making some wrong ones. Go easy on yourself. In this period, success is just doing better today than you did yesterday. You will succeed when you make realistic goals: just one small noticeable difference in your responses today from yesterday, or even this month from last month.

Change can, and often does, take time and patience. Transformational change obeys the laws of nature, where great things take time. The commitment to change is a lifelong process. Permanent change takes patience and perseverance. You must not only know what to change, you must sense when to change and adapt to the new experience of acting differently. You are working toward the person you want to be, and your progress will often be two steps forward and one step back. You can't afford to waste time or energy on self-blame and doubt. Remember the muscle tissue metaphor. You are building new muscles and it will take time to develop and strengthen the muscle fibers.

All the shifts you experience as you learn to skillfully play your particular hand in life will propel you into the next stage of healing, "Getting It Together: Healing Yourself." You no longer automatically react to the circumstances in which you find yourself, but increasingly respond from your intentions and love.

—ⱱ—

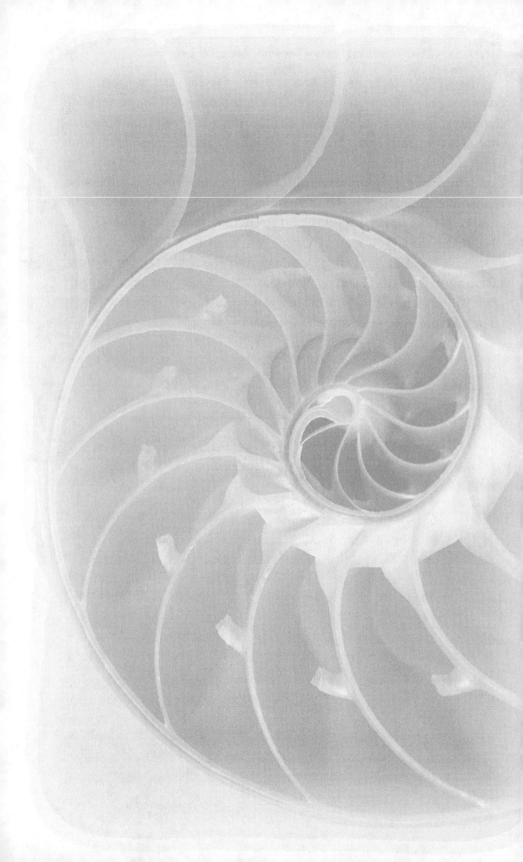

CHAPTER 6

Getting It Together—Healing Yourself and Finding Happiness

—⚒—

What Does "Getting It Together" Mean?

More than simply an ownership of problems as in "core issues" and more than a movement away from the influence of OCD as in "moving beyond," this stage unfolds with each moment you move toward your own healing and embrace active responsibility for yourself. With the freedom that results when you move beyond the spell of OCD comes a greater responsibility to include yourself in the healing process. You are moving *toward* a proactive stance of living in which you take control of your life through the vision, mission, commitments, and promises you make to yourself and others.

In this stage you focus on *your* wounding, *your* betrayal, *your* heroism, and *your* journey. Like other survivors who are triumphant and go on to greater understanding and acceptance, you reappraise your life, reorder your values and priorities, recreate meaningful relationships, and restore broken connections. This stage ushers in a consciousness and reverence toward life that transcends the wounding from OCD. In the words of the poet James Hastings, "The needle that pierces may carry a thread that bonds us to heaven." No longer suffering without meaning, you move from victimization to heroism and from small and circumscribed views of your life to finding your unique place in the great web of life.

"Getting it together" occurs when the war within is over. An African proverb states, "You can outdistance that which is running after you, but you cannot outdistance that which is running inside you." When you stop comparing your inner self to everyone's outer self, you discover that we all have some burdens with which we must cope. You begin to appreciate that some burdens are actually worse than OCD, such as terminal cancer or multiple sclerosis. And some burdens are easier than OCD. In the larger perspective, OCD is just one of a number of problems or wounds that can befall us. In addition, having OCD certainly offers no immunity to life's other wounds. They often co-exist, just as a person can have the measles and a broken wrist at the same time.

Roy C. captures the essence of getting it together in his survival guide for families when he writes, "OCD doesn't end life, it redirects it." At this stage of healing, the direction is conscious and chosen. By assuming responsibility for yourself, you feel a greater sense of control or coherency in your life. Getting it together involves, in the mythic or legendary sense, the descent into your own cave of darkness to do battle with your own demons, whether they are your expectations, your failed dreams, or a host of other losses and shocks. The OCD can be like any monster or dragon that threatens your realm, or home. It is heroic and noble to create a life of grace and joy in spite of its presence.

The scientific literature on well-being points to what we can do to put more effectiveness into our lives and, therefore, get it together. Summarizing thousands of research articles,[44] eminent researcher David Myers, whom we met in the preceding chapter, reports that well-being results from the following steps: develop fit and healthy bodies; acquire realistic expectations; build self-esteem; create a strong sense of control and direction in one's life; become outgoing; cultivate supportive friendships that enable companionship and confiding; maintain a socially intimate, sexually warm, equitable marriage; find challenging work and active leisure, punctuated by adequate rest and retreat; and exercise a faith that involves communal support, purpose, and acceptance.[44]

There is no magic to achieving these steps. While some people learn them more easily than others or might have less to learn, most of us can develop them to create a more satisfying and meaningful life. Cognitive-behavioral therapy teaches that simply going through the motions of well-being can trigger the feelings of well-being. When you want to change in any of the above areas, like increasing self-esteem or becoming more optimistic and assertive, begin by doing the various behaviors associated with each step even if you feel you are merely acting the role. If you want to experience more control in your life, act as if the choices you make are important. If you want to exercise more faith, make time to pray or read inspiring spiritual materials. Fortunately, even when you don't feel like it, faking it can work. Pretend self-esteem. Feign optimism. Simulate "outgoingness." And as you do, you may find a new attitude growing in you.

I have a mentor who often says life is a game. You are either on the court or in the stands—you are either a player or a bystander. The choice is yours! "Getting it together" means you suit up and choose to play—again and again and again. Churchill's immortal words, "Never, never, never, never give up," apply here as well. In periods in which you are together, you accept that the OCD is a part of your game, too, but only one part. The OCD is no longer seen as a wrong path in the road of your life. *It is an integral part of your road.*

A major transition to becoming a player occurs when you successfully renegotiate your expectations. Your expectations provide the boundaries of the game in which you play. Changing your expectations, therefore, changes your life. To start, clearly and precisely define what your current expectations are. You may think that this step is unnecessary because you believe you know them well. In guiding others like you through this exercise, however, I have found that almost everyone discovers that they are expecting things of themselves and others of which they are completely unaware. So, write down the phrase: "I expect that my partner (child, parent, lover, sibling, or friend) will...." Finish this sentence stem twenty-five times for each of the above that apply.

Next, write things you remember your parents telling you about this particular type of relationship. Include those that still apply in your expectations, even if ever so slightly. Recall any myths, stories, or fantasies you believed as a child or believe now.

Finally, review each expectation and decide which ones are realistic and attainable in your life now. This information provides the boundaries of the life you lead. Now that you know more about the life you have been leading, you have the opportunity to discard those expectations that no longer serve you, readjust the boundaries of your life, and choose to live more consciously. This seemingly simple exercise can have a powerful effect on your life—and ultimately the lives of your loved ones.

It is important to clarify that getting it together is not about being perfect. It's also not about having it all together. There is a funny aphorism that states, "I finally got it all together but I forgot where I put it." Essentially, getting it together is about healing. Healing is not an absence of problems but rather an increasing ability to handle problems in better ways. What was difficult if not impossible before, you can now do with more and more facility.

Finally, this stage is characterized by integrity. There is an inner alignment. Your thoughts, feelings, behaviors, intentions, and goals are consistent. You no longer think one thing, feel another, and do something else, none of which are in accord. The expression "your collar and cuffs match" is very fitting for this stage of healing. In the language of 12-Step programs, you "walk your talk" instead of "talk your walk." You not only say that you matter, for example, but you behave as if you do and engage in behaviors consistent with taking care of yourself. You choose self-care by engaging in life-enhancing behaviors like exercising, meditating, painting, walking, hiking, or relaxing. Steven Covey,[14] whose book *The Seven Habits of Highly Successful People* has sold more than ten million copies, calls this set of skills "sharpening the saw." You will not go far without self-care.

What Promotes Getting It Together?

An article in the 1997 *Journal of the California Alliance for the Mentally Ill* describes a special project called "The Journey of Hope," which has already reached out to more than twenty thousand family members of the mentally ill in thirty-five states. It was first developed in 1991 by the Louisiana Alliance for the Mentally Ill. It is based upon "an empowerment model nourished by our belief in the inherent strength of families and our pride in their proven capabilities as teachers." A family-to-family self-help support and education program, it lists "10 principles of support." These principles, which were written by Louisiana families who developed and fostered the JOH, summarize so much of what is being said in this book and are so central to healing from OCD that I will list them.

1. We acknowledge and accept the fact that someone we love has a mental illness.

2. We accept that we have no control over this illness or the individual with the illness. We only have control over our own actions and thoughts.

3. We release all feelings of guilt concerning this mental illness for we are not to blame for the illness or its effects.

4. We understand and acknowledge that the mental illness has had an impact on all of our relationships.

5. We forgive ourselves for the mistakes we have made and we forgive others for wrongs we feel have been committed against us.

6. We choose to be happy and healthy. We choose to return to a healthy focus on ourselves.

7. We keep our expectations for ourselves and for our mentally ill loved ones at realistic levels.

8. We believe that we have inner resources which will help us with our own growth and will sustain us through crisis.

9. We acknowledge the strength and value of this support system and we commit ourselves to sustaining it for our benefit and the benefit of other families.

10. We acknowledge that there is a higher power to whom we will turn to nurture and strengthen our ability to release those things we cannot control.

"Getting it together" embodies these important principles. We can progress only so far without a belief system anchored in these principles.

What Is Healing?

The art and science of healing are consistent in concluding that healing is similar whether it pertains to the mind, body, or soul. Whether a wound is torn flesh or a shattered spirit, the healing process is similar and occurs because nature is intelligent. It is nature's inherent program to re-establish contact and connection with you, others, and the greater story of which you are a part. When healing, you experience wholeness through stronger connections with the mind, body, soul, and spirit. Healing maintains the active interplay among all three.

There are many ways to define healing.[26] Dictionary definitions emphasize that healing is the process of becoming whole again. Medically, healing occurs when we are "all well" and "not ill" anymore. Energetically, healing is compared to restoring the energy flow. Eastern or psychospiritual traditions view healing as a balancing of opposing forces or a harmonizing of disparate voices, images, or conflicts. Whenever there is separateness, healing is blocked. From a shamanistic perspective, healing is the reclamation of the lost parts of the soul. All definitions of healing agree that it occurs when we are resonating and connecting with the deeper and wiser parts of the self.

Healing can be an initiation that ushers in greater capacities and possibilities. It establishes relationships that did not exist before. It embodies the principle that the highest form of creativity is to sculpt your own life. Not simply a return to previous functioning, healing is an alignment with who we truly are. Because all parts of the self are accepted, healing is accepting "what is." It occurs when there is no resistance to what is. Imagine your struggle in life if you resisted breathing, sleeping, or eating.

In terms of the influence of OCD, healing means there is an end to the war within. You surrender to and accept the fact that your loved one has OCD. You stop resisting and stop protesting. In the process, you identify your own limits, set limits for others, and you take back the essence of who you are. Healing is letting go of fear and embracing love, forgiving, becoming free of judgment, expectation, and control.

Healing is a process leading to health, not an event. It is more than the absence of injury, illness, or dysfunction. Healing involves connectedness, love, compassion, acceptance, and surrender. It is associated with living spaciously, consciously, heroically, and finding the universal in the personal. It unfolds as a person makes six key transitions in life. Each transition opens the door to further healing. In another book, *Trauma and Adversity: Triumph's Crucible* (2006), I will examine the following six journeys in the healing process in great depth.

1. "The Journey from Addiction to Spaciousness"—the transition from bondage and slavery to freedom and openness.

2. "The Journey from Shame to Self-Esteem"—the transition from believing that you are worthless at the core to an experience of your own inner preciousness.

3. "The Journey from Unconscious to Conscious Living"—the transition from refusing to accept responsibility to choosing countless times a day the state of consciousness in which you wish to be.

4. "The Journey from Victim to Hero"—the transition from seeing yourself as helpless and out of control to one of taking charge of your life.

5. "The Journey from Personalization to Universalization"—the transition from taking OCD personally (even though you are personally affected) to the realization that OCD is only one part of a larger cosmic drama.

6. "The Journey from a Newtonian to a Quantum Worldview"—the transition from a linear, cause-and-effect model of reality to the richly interconnected quantum world of the new physics.

When you actively and daily incorporate these six core transitions,[26] you are healing. In order to reach a healing threshold, however, you must develop a practice or discipline that incorporates one or more of these on a daily basis. Getting everything you want is not the culmination of your healing, nor does healing necessarily spring from a sense of abundance. The mind, given free reign, perpetually generates a lifetime of wants and desires and is never fully satisfied. The practice of abundance is not about how much you can get. Rather, it arises when you feel that whatever you have is enough.

What Is the Difference Between Healing and Curing?

The distinction between healing and curing is crucial to further understanding OCD. Not long ago I had a cold. I took aspirin and the appropriate amount of chicken soup. In short order I was cured. There was no evidence anywhere in my body of that cold. All symptoms were gone. Lab tests would have confirmed that there was no longer any trace of illness in my body. When cured, our bodies and minds return to their previous state. There has been no fundamental change or shift.

But we are never fully cured of our traumatic wounds. In contrast to curing, our traumatic wounds may or may not be eliminated when we heal. But suffering is gone. We discover we are not separate but are part of the unity of the universe. Healing goes deeper than symptoms; it involves becoming clear about our real self and purpose in life. We realize that dying isn't the worst outcome. There are some things that are worse than death.

Dying, in this context, could be a healing, the end to a full, rich life for someone who is weary and in need of rest. Or, healing could mean spending the rest of your life in a wheelchair—if that's how you can best perform your life's task. The successful healing process, therefore, does not necessarily produce comfort, ease, or prolonged life. Rather it produces a clear vision of who we need to be and the strength and integration of mind, body, and spirit to be that person regardless of what happens to or around us. It is the truth that heals, but initially it can make us angry. There are times we may regret setting foot on this path because it doesn't necessarily make life easier. But it does make it better. One of my client's summarized this sentiment, "One moment of recovery is worth a lifetime of suffering."

Aren't You the Healthy One? Are You in Need of Healing?

A constant theme throughout this book is that OCD is a family illness. Many sources of help minimize or ignore the healing of family and loved ones. Because OCD has the potential to affect everyone under its influence, the distinction of healing described in this book is that it is for the entire family affected by OCD.

Having a loved one with OCD is a major loss, as we have seen in earlier chapters. Yet loss is a natural part of life. Whether the experience is a positive, soul-filled one or a negative, self-diminishing one depends on how the family responds to its loss. And therein lies the key. In many families, the loss itself can become the primary trauma, not the OCD. The actual problem may not even be the illness, or the OCD sufferer, *but how you are reacting.* Until now you may have thought it was the other person who caused you to feel the way you do. Now you come to realize that you are in control of your own life.

It is safe to assume you have been affected by OCD. The questions are how, when, and to what degree have you been affected? Some people are so affected that they need professional help themselves. Others need just a little guidance. When in doubt, seek professional consultation. Because we need healing doesn't necessarily mean we need treatment or therapy.

What Is the Relationship Between Healing and Love?

Love may be the common denominator that underlies all successful healing. Without it, there can be no true healing. True healing involves connection: connection with self, or self-love; connection with another, or intimacy; and connection with something beyond, or spirituality. Love is the driving force behind healing. Its absence or subjugation leads to problems. Studies on institutionalized infants have shown that those infants who were not loved did not do as well as others in motor, emotional, intellectual, and behavioral development. For example, in a classic study René Spitz found that children who spent their first year in institutions would lie or sit with expressionless eyes and frozen, immobile faces. Spitz called this cluster of behaviors "anaclitic depression." Other studies confirm the harmful effects of the early loss of love.

A cursory view of the healing literature thrusts the whole notion of love into the recovery equation. Karl Menninger, one of the first psychiatrists to address the nature of love in healing, states, "It is this intangible thing, love; love in many forms, which enters into every therapeutic [healing] relationship. It is an element of which the physician may be the carrier, the vessel. And it is an element which binds and heals, which comforts and restores, which works what we have to call—for now—miracles." The essence of psychoanalysis is the analysis of the transference relationship between patient and therapist where the patient experiences a successful love relationship.

One of the most widely known proponents of love in healing, M. Scott Peck,[47] states, "In short, the essential ingredient of successful deep and meaningful psychotherapy is love." He boldly asserts, "...it is essential for the therapist to love a patient for the therapy to be successful, and if the therapy does become successful, then the therapeutic relationship will become a mutually loving one." If the therapist cannot love the patient, says Peck, "genuine healing will not occur," regardless of how well-trained and learned the therapist is!

Love, says Peck, is not to be confused with romantic or sexual involvement. It is not a dependency upon another, nor is it easy. On the contrary, love requires commitment and work. Love is full of effort—it is "the will to extend one's self for the purpose of nurturing one's own or another's spiritual growth." To extend one's self means go out on a limb; to get emotionally involved; to struggle in there with the other person. It is a self-replenishing activity, and genuine love always enlarges one's self.

Research has shown that the effects of love on the body can be measured.[26] Numerous studies show the beneficial effects of love on survival rates, longevity, the immune system, and other basic biological processes. For example, husbands whose wives kiss them goodbye in the morning have fewer auto accidents and live an average of five years longer.

Richard Moss in *The I That is We*[1] wrote, "By embracing unconditional love [love without expectation or condition] you surrender all emotions and thoughts that separate you from well-being and harmony." When expressing our love, we are extending the truest, fullest, and most powerful energy within us. Love is a creative power through which we extend our very essence. Love is the power that focuses its light on the darkest, most shadowy parts of ourselves.

What all of this means for OCD is relatively simple: to heal from OCD, the sufferer must be exposed to, *and feel*, the love of those around him or her. Without this love, recovery will be slow, difficult, or perhaps impossible. The person must experience what it means to be valued and prized-even though he or she may have OCD. In essence, love goes a long way. As Phyllis Diller once said, "A smile is a curve that straightens everything out."

What Are the Characteristics of People Who Heal?

We all know people who are rarely defeated or embittered by their circumstances. Even the most devastating situations do not break them. They have faced death; they have faced horrible conditions and environments; and they have faced their inner demons and devils. Such people leave footprints that we can follow. They are inspirational and their incredible resourcefulness and feats of heart and soul remind us of what we, too, can do. They are as relevant to those healing from the influence of OCD as any other affliction.

By studying what one chronicler calls "triumphant survivors," we glimpse the thoughts, the feelings, the behaviors, and the spirit of those who heal from traumas of all kinds, including OCD. They serve as models. We can learn to strengthen ourselves by adopting their manner of dealing with difficulties. When we apply their practices to our own situations, we too move from the ordinary to the extraordinary.

Certain characteristics of survivors of all types of traumas tend to be mentioned over and over.[22,26,55] Of course, not every survivor has all or even a majority of the characteristics mentioned in the following list:

1. Survivors have the commitment to survive.

2. Embedded within this intention of the survivor are the convictions that stumbling blocks can be stepping stones and failures are the rungs on the ladder of success. Survivors would agree with the Zen Buddhist aphorism, "Challenge is the correct way to view an inconvenience, and inconvenience is the incorrect way to view a challenge."

3. Survivors view life as an extended, unfolding process and experience life's events as just another chapter in a very long book that is continually being written. They do not draw premature conclusions based on a few chapters.

4. Survivors respond as if every event in life has meaning and their task is to discover or create that meaning. They believe that they may not fully know the meaning of an event or circumstance for years and are willing to wait.

5. Survivors have an instinctive belief that it is not so much the event that is important as how they respond to it. They know they have little or no control over the event and much more control over their own actions.

6. Survivors feel connected to something larger than themselves, whether it is God, nature, a tree, or a group. They have a love for others and a desire to improve the human condition. They believe in the dignity and value of human life. They have a respect for nature, the planet, and its residents.

7. Survivors know how to grieve and say goodbye and ritualize their loss in a ceremony, like a Jewish Shiva or a Christian wake.

8. Survivors have a sense of humor and can laugh at themselves and the predicaments in which they find themselves.

9. Survivors readily ask for help and treat those who help them well. They find positive role models to emulate and inspire them.

10. Survivors accept full personal responsibility for what happens and do not blame others or themselves. They do not complain. They are willing to work hard and accept that all progress is two steps forward and one step backward.

11. Survivors tell their story again and again to trustworthy people.

12. Survivors know that circumstances reveal character and do not determine it.

Are There Other Benefits You Can Look Forward to in Your Healing?

Illness and trauma can both birth healing.[22,39] Healing in turn begets excellence. In fact, trauma can be a special vessel, or crucible for excellence. Excellence is one of those words that is more easily recognized than described. It can be defined as much by what it's not as by what it is. Excellence is not a "thing" and so cannot be measured or possessed. One of my teachers used to say, "Excellence is knowing the right thing to do, having the will to do it, and enough talent and ability to carry it through." When practicing excellence, you actively seek conscious, intimate connection with yourself, others, and something beyond yourself.

Henry David Thoreau once stated, "I know of no more encouraging fact than the unquestionable ability of man to elevate his life by conscious desire." As such, excellence is always a triumph of directed consciousness and the realization of your conscious ideals through self mastery.

Excellence is not limited to a chosen few. You can achieve it. Nor does excellence mean you have it all together. Having it all together is as unrealistic as eating once and never again. Excellence is the commitment to having it together one more time than not. It requires the commitment to triumph over adversity. It is, therefore, a component of "getting it together."

How Are Healing and Excellence Different?

Excellence and healing share much in common and often go hand in hand. Despite their similarities, there is value in distinguishing them. True excellence[26] occurs after healing occurs. While the primary focus of healing is dealing with injury, the primary focus of excellence is on the development of the self, which leads to well-being. Excellence is the ability to hold all of life's joys and sorrows, and let neither take you off the court of life. Churchill once said that "power is the ability to move from failure to failure with enthusiasm." The same can be said of excellence. Whatever is happening becomes grist for the mill of our next step.

Life can be likened to a wave. The wave goes up and the wave goes down. There are highs and there are lows. How you *deal with* the wave is the essence of excellence. Some get fooled and believe that excellence is the *right* wave. Every wave is the right wave for the person of excellence. When you ride the wave well, you get up quickly when you lose your balance. When you fall, you don't make excuses about falling that imply something is wrong with you or the wave. You also fall less and less. As you progress, you recover more quickly from life's mishaps.

What Is the Relationship Between Trauma and Excellence?

Trauma and excellence may seem like strange bedfellows, but they are necessary ones in "getting it together." Throughout time we have known that while hardship brings pain, it is also a testing ground for strength, courage, and an appreciation for life's simple things. We seldom tap into our deepest strengths and abilities until forced to do so. This self-evident truth is expressed in science, psychology, and philosophy.[26,63]

Experts in human resilience point out that falling apart is less an unfortunate event than a prelude to renewal. Falling apart and putting the pieces together in a new form is a central theme throughout all nature, including in the human life cycle. Disruption and then reintegration are often a necessary prelude to personal development also. Ilya Prigogone, the Nobel Prize chemist, demonstrated the capacity of systems to regenerate to higher levels of self-organization in response to environmental stress. Chaos can be a time of creativity and opportunity.

Psychologist James Hillman described problems as the soul's way of working on itself. In his comments about psychologically healthy people, Abraham Maslow, who is often called the father of the human potential movement, referred to the "continental divide" principle. He said, "I use this principle to describe the fact that stress will either break people altogether if they are, in the beginning, too weak to stand distress, or else, if they are already strong enough to take stress in the first place, the same stress, if they come through it, will strengthen them, temper them, and make them stronger."

In a similar way, the philosopher Nietzsche said, "What doesn't kill us strengthens us." Philosopher Martin Buber said, "All suffering prepares the soul for vision."

If necessity is the mother of invention, then pain may be the father of excellence. Pain and suffering are not exceptions to the human condition; they are the human condition. Wounding becomes a crucible of excellence when new meanings are forged from old circumstances. Trauma as a crucible for excellence is more than the alchemist's notion of turning lead into gold. It is choosing to embrace trauma as an awakening, through words, images, feelings, and deeds.

People who have moved from trauma to excellence[26] are those who have met the following five specific criteria:

1. They must have experienced a major wound, crisis, adversity, loss or disappointment.

2. They must have survived.

3. They have moved through the crisis as a result of personal effort, using their good sense and wisdom.

4. They have emerged with previously unknown strengths and abilities.

5. They have found value in the experience and have discovered a beneficial outcome.

Excellence, therefore, can be seen as the natural result of the following:

1. Welcoming, expecting, and meeting adversity head on.

2. Stretching beyond your current life by recognizing and avoiding the negative spells in your life.

3. Feeling all your feelings, especially laughing and crying, without having them affect you adversely.

4. Asking coping questions that advance your commitments. Questions such as the following are especially helpful: "What would be useful for me to do right now?" "Tomorrow?" "What is the loving thing to do now?" "Do I want to be right or happy?" "Who do I want to be in this situation?"

5. Asking questions that suggest a positive result. For example, "Why is it good that this happened?" "Where is the opportunity I didn't see before?" "What could I do to turn this around and have it turn out well for me?"

6. Living playfully with a curious attitude.

7. Following through. There is a strong drive in us toward completion. If we say we are going to do something and don't do it, a part of our mind remains preoccupied and, therefore, tied up with the incompletion until we clear it.

8. Avoiding all-or-none functioning. Black and white is the world of extremes. It lives more in our minds than in the outer world.

9. Developing an attitude of gratitude. The famous Swiss psychiatrist Carl Jung once said, "I never met a grateful neurotic."

10. Making a commitment to live each day with courage, passion, and love.

What Is the Course of Excellence?

Life unfolds like an interactive video game where every time you become proficient at one level of play, the computer presents you with the next level of difficulty. Of course, as soon as you master that level, you are ushered immediately into the next. In order to win, you must traverse a path of progressively more and more difficult tasks. Similarly, the course of excellence challenges the creative powers of the human mind.

The development of excellence[26] progressively cycles through the following four stages that we met at the end of Chapter Four.

1. "Unconscious incompetence." In this stage, you don't even know enough to know you can't manage something or know that something is wrong. This closely resembles the stage of denial.

2. "Conscious incompetence." Now, at least, you realize that something is wrong and you are involved in some way. This is the beginning of liberation. This is your call to learn something new.

3. "Conscious competence." You can now recognize the need for a particular skill and consciously summon it. You know, for example, that situations such as needing to restrain yourself from enabling call for warrior-like energy. With effort, you can deliver the necessary amount of that energy. You have acquired the skill.

4. "Unconscious competence" is the hallmark of mastery. In this stage, you no longer have to devote conscious attention to areas that once demanded enormous amounts of your time and energy. Remember when you learned to drive a car? Remember how much energy it took?

The more skill areas in which you are unconsciously competent, the more free you are to learn and master other areas. This state of integration or wholeness has been called many things, including bliss, nirvana, samadi, and God consciousness. In the language of traumatic stress, we have "re-integrated" the disconnected self. In mythic language, we are living the "larger story," devoid of strong negative trances. An entrepreneur speaks of the habits of effective people, of mission, and of accountability.

A course in excellence must always address the endemic nature of adversity in all of our lives. Being ordinary is to avoid whatever situation or circumstance that brought us adversity. Being extraordinary is to embrace all that is happening as just what needs to be happening to develop to the next step of growth. In other words, adversity is to be neither avoided nor dreaded. Rather, it is to be confronted, expected, and utilized. The essential attitude toward all life's offerings is the refrain "Yes/and" rather than "Yes/but," that all too familiar refrain of victimization.

The course of excellence is always one of course correction. Like the pilot flying an airplane from one coast to another, you are constantly correcting course, bringing your aircraft back to its proper direction to complete your mission.

What Does Mythology Have to Offer in Healing From OCD?

The *American Heritage Dictionary* defines mythology as "a collection of myths about the origin and history of a people and their Gods, ancestors, and heroes." Myths—the folk stories, fairy tales, fables, and legends that have been passed down through all of time—provide rich glimpses into our ancestral heritage and our future possibilities. Understanding the universal themes and patterns suggested by mythology provides a useful, practical map of the healing process. The old stories of initiation and heroic journeys bring forth the concept of the sacred, the context in which all transformations occur.

So, let your imagination roam. Because myths illuminate the inner workings of the psyche, looking at life through a mythological lens can deepen your understanding of trauma and healing. As clues to the spiritual potentials of life, myths broaden horizons and offer guidance from the accumulated past. Today's pain becomes linked with people who have gone before and connects us to all the great rhythms and cycles of life. Imparting the great truths of all times, myths transport us beyond the local, limited, and immediate circumstances of our personal history to view our real place in the great web of life.

When we live mythically,[10] we find life is always much bigger than our particular circumstance. The mythological perspective elevates our local stories to a higher, different level. We see ourselves as part of a progression, and we glimpse the epic struggle as we cope with OCD. Heroism and discipline cast a bright light on the journey.

A mythological lens[26] offers an alternative to blame, revenge, and self pity. Although rarely comfortable, seldom easy, and not even always a "safe" alternative, a mythical perspective allows us to engage in the larger story that connects us to universal patterns. When we are disconnected from the sacred, we fall victim to tyranny by our local, historical, or psychological story. As long as we are connected only to our small story, as long as this is our *only* story, we will seek to "understand" our suffering through self-condemnation, addiction, and quick cures.

We need new stories. The best stories are agents of the sacred and therefore of healing. Through these stories we understand the complexities faced by others. We need stories to heal the polarization that can overwhelm us, to connect us with each other, and to calm those of us who are frightened. Bestselling author and psychotherapist Mary Pipher[48] reminds us that, "quilted together, these stories will shelter us all."

What Does Mythology Say About Heroism?

Myth teaches that it is our nature to be heroic! Heroism is the journey to find the Grail of the true self and bring it back to the ones you love. Heroes find the larger story in their own wounds and, in the process, make their wounds sacred. Many writers from Carl Jung to mythologist Joseph Campbell describe the hero/heroine path. According to Jung, "The hero's [heroine's] main feat is to overcome the monster of darkness: it is the long-hoped-for and expected triumph of consciousness over the unconscious." As Campbell writes in his classic book, *The Hero With a Thousand Faces,* "The hero...is the man or woman who has been able to battle past his personal and local historical limitations to the generally valid, normally human forms."

The hero's journey[10] always begins with the hero leaving home and separating from the powerful pull or trance of the family. Destiny is summoning us. From a mythical perspective, we respond to a "call to adventure." If we refuse the call, we remain stuck.

Next, heroes/heroines descend into the nether world to encounter the "road of trials." Here, the hero/heroine is presented with tests and tasks. The voyager now must survive a succession of trials, although the hero is covertly helped, in Campbell's words,[10] by "the advice, amulets, and secret agents" of a "benign power." This is the process of transcending or transmuting our personal past. In mythic terms, heroes and heroines enter the cave of their core issues and dispel the false truths of childhood, slay inner dragons, fight demons, find the treasure, or receive a blessing or gift.

Having descended deep into the personal caves of transformation and integration, the hero must still return home with the treasures found. To complete the adventure, the hero/heroine must survive the impact of the world. Mythology teaches us that this is the hero's ultimate difficult task. In the completion, heroes form a new relationship with truth, courage, love, and pain.

The late actor Christopher Reeve, who starred in the "Superman" movies, broke his neck in a freak horse accident and was paralyzed. During his healing process, he launched a one-man publicity and lobbying campaign to help *all* people with spinal cord injuries. The make-believe Superman became a real-life one as he began a new and different life. Christopher Reeve was just one visible example of the super hero in all of us and the healing that is inherent in our nature. Actor Marc Summers and other intrepid and brave souls like him who publicly acknowledge their OCD do much to take this illness out of the shadows, and they are also heroes to be admired.

Heroes and heroines accept that they were never meant to be completely satisfied. They have faith that the truth will set them free, but they also know that first it may make them miserable. They have a willingness to tolerate anxiety and uncertainty in the pursuit of goals. The hero and heroine accept the process of struggle as part of life, even the darkest moments of anguish. This acceptance is also one of the most important attitudes that differentiates individuals with high self-esteem from those with low self-esteem.

The hero/heroine dares to love because he or she knows love is the ultimate and highest goal to which we can aspire. The hero/heroine knows each one of us was created to love and be loved. Daring to love is in itself an act of heroism. The hero/heroine learns to understand his or her place in world—the hero/heroine learns that it is not *his* or *her* pain that must be confronted but it is *the* pain that must be confronted and transformed.[2,26,39]

What Kind of a Trauma Is OCD From a Mythic Viewpoint?

From a mythic perspective, the making of the soul begins with the wounding of the psyche by the Larger Story.[31] Some aspect of our being propels us forward and the psyche is opened. Trauma becomes the invitation: a larger story is revealed by the wounding. This wounding tells us that old forms are ready to go. It creates the holes in the soul through which light pours, and the wounding becomes an invitation to your own renaissance. "The wounding becomes sacred," writes mythologist Jean Houston, "when we are willing to release our old stories and to become the vehicles through which the new story may emerge into time." A sacred wound opens a person to healing.

It is only out of challenge that the higher aspects of life emerge. By understanding trauma as a process of initiation to individual and collective excellence, trauma becomes a sacred wound, a wound leading you to deeper connections with yourself, others, and something greater. Healings seem to require understanding of your deepest wounds. So it is that healers go through a necessary state of wounding.

The motif of the "wounded healer" is universal and appears in every culture. Recovering alcoholics and other addicts serve as wounded healers, calling others to a life of serenity. Those who face illness, catastrophe, and even death often report that the experience gave them renewed meaning and purpose. The master hypnotist Milton Erickson said his polio, color blindness, and tone deafness fostered his remarkable enjoyment of life and his ability to help others.

How Do You Grieve or Mourn Your Wounds?

The better question is "How have you learned *not* to grieve?" Grieving is an instinctive process. All you have to do is to get out of its way. All animals engage in it. Unlike other animals, however, the key to grieving and mourning for human beings is that it is an interpersonal act. This means that to grieve effectively (i.e., in a healing manner), you must share your grief with at least one other person and be able to look into that person's eyes and know that he or she understands your wound.

Mourning is simply a process of communicating the many feelings you have over your loss. Grieving occurs naturally as you tell your story about what happened to you—what you lost, what you gave up, what you missed out on, what you might never see, and what can never be. Grieving hurts; it comes from deep inside the belly. It is no fun. But it allows you to go on with your life.

Unlike grieving that follows a single event, like a death, your grieving the losses to OCD may be constant—it can go on and on. In some ways, this makes it harder for you. Also, you probably will not get the aid, comfort, and support that others may get when they lose someone close. Your process of grieving, therefore, is one that you may need to return to again and again.

There are four general tasks in grieving your loss.

1. Stop denying and accept the reality of the loss.

2. Work through the pain of grief by expressing it to at least one other person.

3. Adjust to living a life without that which has been lost.

4. Withdraw the energy previously invested in the past and invest it in your present and your future.

All of these are relatively simple steps; they just are not at all easy. Be gentle with yourself and allow yourself the honor and dignity of whatever time and manner your grief requires. Everyone is different. Some cry; some get angry; some transfer their sadness into a cause or into work. There is not one correct way.

Can You Inadvertently Sabotage Yourself?

You will, on occasion, slip back into old unproductive behaviors like blame, enabling, abandonment, rage, or a host of others. You will make mistakes. You will need to constantly correct your course toward healing in order to arrive at your destination. Most journeys are not a straight line, and you will often find yourself straying from your path. The task is to recognize when you are sabotaging yourself, stop, correct your course, and get back on track. You will also begin to reduce the time between sabotaging events. Your progress will be in an upward direction, but don't be surprised if you may circle back sometimes. Remember, even when you fall flat on your face, you are moving forward. Success is defined as getting up one more time than you fall down.

What Kind of Relationship Can You Have With the Person With OCD?

What kind of relationship do you want? Who do you want to be and how do you want to treat those you love? The person with OCD deserves love, too. It's from this place that you can really envision and create the relationship that you want. Whether it's being a better parent, better spouse, or deciding to leave, you are now in a position to determine your important relationships, rather than only reacting to what's going on around you.

You may still experience some guilt as you practice new ways of relating and responding. It's important to remember that you used to feel guilty because you couldn't control the person with OCD. Now you may feel guilty because you feel better and behave in new ways. This new guilt is part of the process and is temporary. As you continue to take care of yourself and change your patterns of behavior, you actually improve your relationships, even though initially it may not seem that way. You, the person with OCD, and the rest of the family may find these changes unsettling. But as these new behaviors lead to healthier and improved relationships, the sense of doing things wrong diminishes and you find it easier to do what was once guilt-producing.

Ultimately, the kind of relationship you can have with the person with OCD largely depends upon what you want it to be. Even when the person with OCD doesn't cooperate, you have much more control of *yourself* and *your* reactions than you might first believe. It's an inside job, one you accomplish yourself, rather than an outside job, or one dependent on circumstances and the health of the person with OCD. It requires you to live from your commitments and not your feelings. You're in the driver's seat now, not the OCD. While this is certainly not an easy task, it is one that can be done.

Will OCD Cease to Be a Problem?

Alas, no. But it ceases to be big trouble. Mark Twain said it best, "Life is one damn thing after another; trouble is the same damn thing again and again." The OCD always requires your time and attention. You get better and better at recognizing danger signals early and effectively responding to them quickly and powerfully. Because OCD can wax and wane, it just waits for you to get sloppy and forget all that you have learned.

What Feelings Predominate in This Stage?

The predominant feelings that characterize this stage are wholeness, calmness, and peace. You are able to accept your circumstances and not fight against them. There is a surrender and acceptance, much like the alcoholic learns to surrender to his or her illness. At this stage, little time is spent cursing the OCD or the person with it.

How Do You Foster This Stage?

Stay open, stay curious, and stay well—physically, emotionally, mentally, and spiritually. This stage, like the others, requires time and energy. The first key to effective change is desire and commitment, and that commitment requires a clear mind. Lifestyle matters such as nutrition, rest, exercise, and meditation all contribute to this clear state of mind and help you to stay on course.

You also want to stay connected to the person with OCD but not connected to the OCD itself. This can be difficult at first. It requires that you see your loved ones *as separate from the OCD*, just as you see yourself separate from them. You love them and want them to know that. This requires practice, but here again the muscle gets stronger as you exercise it.

Is There a Cure for You?

That depends on what you mean by a cure. There is no more a cure for you than there is a cure for life, because living with someone with OCD is a part of your life. You have one slice of the pie of life; somebody else has another. For you, it is OCD; for somebody else it might be a loved one with cancer. There is no safety and no certainty. Uncertainty is what the person with OCD can't live with. You can show that it can be lived with. And not only can it be lived with, you can create a happy, effective, meaningful life from it. OCD expert Jonathan Grayson's diagnostic question to his prospective clients is, "Are you willing to live with uncertainty?" There is often an unconscious wish that doing therapy allows a person to feel certain. Loved ones of OCD sufferers must ask themselves this same question to deal with their unconscious wish. The goal is to live with uncertainty and a minimum of anxiety. Loved ones also must go beyond the "Big Lie" that "in the perfect life there are no problem behaviors, sad events, or failed efforts."

Having a family member with OCD certainly is a trauma. To some families it's a large trauma, but to other families it's a small trauma. The goal is to use the trauma as a challenge, a crucible for excellence. Trite as it may seem, it's helpful to remember that it could always be worse.

Where Does Spirituality Play a Role?

The recovery movement, which reached its pinnacle in the 1980s, attests to the central role of spirituality in healing from addictions as well as obsessions and compulsions. In fact, all 12-Step programs are spiritual. James Callner believes that "Recovery is about pushing through fears, and recovery is about reclaiming what God gave us all, a spirit of humor and lightness, sometimes even when it seems dark." I heard Roy C. define fear as the acronym for Face Everything And Recover.

Father Leo Booth, an icon in the field of spirituality and addictions, defines spirituality in his "letter from the professional community" in the "Big Book" of Obsessive-Compulsive Anonymous as being "that God-given ingredient (given to all human beings, regardless of color, culture, or creed) that enables the development of a positive and creative lifestyle." He adds: "Spirituality reminds us that we were created to create. Therein lies our responsibility. Spirituality is not simply seen in placing our future dependence upon a Higher Power, but rather stresses an understanding of spirituality more as a precious gift from God that requires nourishing and nourishment."

All those who seek to create a positive lifestyle are in the dynamic of spirituality. And spirituality reminds us that we are of God and God doesn't make junk! "What God made is good," says Booth. Guilt, shame, and feelings of victimization only fuel OCD. Like other spiritual teachers, Booth reminds us if we believe "The Lie" that we are not divine, we start behaving that way and become that way.

Spirituality reminds us to keep an eye on the donut and not the hole. It involves a sense of living a part of something mysterious and bigger than ourselves. This view of life enables us not to get lost in the individual circumstance, or small story, but to see ourselves connected to something larger, the Larger Story. We can't be whole and healthy unless we connect with something beyond our own needs and well-being and happiness.

The Journal of the California Alliance for the Mentally Ill publishes enlightening articles on the spirit of healing. It contains countless stories of people who find great meaning and relief in awakening spiritually. For example, in one of their issues focusing on OCD, Caroline Case wrote: "I wouldn't wish Obsessive-Compulsive Disorder on anyone, but lately I find myself in the curious position of having to be grateful for it. After long, painful years in which obsessions ruled my life, OCD forced me to admit that I was on the wrong path. Today I find myself on a new path, a path of spiritual growth in which my whole approach to life is undergoing a dramatic change."

Christina Dubowski, founder and executive director of the Trichotillomania Learning Center, wrote in a similar vein: "I practice, on a daily basis, the techniques I have developed to cope with impulses to pull [my hair]. I take time to meditate and pray, and attempt to embrace the wild puller within me. For I have accepted that, if this is my 'spiritual homework,' I need to study and learn so as to go on to the next lesson."[15]

Echoing out from the halls of most spiritual paths, whether 12-Step or other, is the belief that "My worst day in recovery is better than my best day obsessing." As said in 12-Step programs, "Keep coming back. It works." That is a wise statement.

What Are the Pitfalls of a Spiritual Approach?

The major pitfall of a spiritual approach is not doing the necessary work. One of the principles of Alcoholics Anonymous, which uses a spiritual approach to learning to live with the disease of alcoholism, is to "turn it over." In other words, when you come up against something that seems insurmountable (like OCD), you turn it over to a power greater than yourself. The danger, however, is in turning it over too soon. Instead, you must turn it over only after you've done your 100 percent about the problem or the situation. Then you "let go and let God." So using spirituality too soon, before you've done the hard work of recovery and healing, is an avoidance device, a way of not accepting responsibility and not dealing with the circumstances you're given.

After You Do Your Work What Should You Do When Your Loved One Engages in a Ritual or Compulsion?

Getting it together is getting control over your own behavior—not controlling the person with OCD. Therefore, there are a number of helpful behaviors in which you might engage. First, remember that breakdowns are natural and inevitable and are to be expected. Your loved ones will engage in OCD behaviors regardless of what you do. It is their illness, not your illness. Second, put the OCD episodes in proportion. Third, view each new episode as an opportunity to move to the next level. Use them to instruct you about where your work is to be done.

Remember to keep your boundaries clear.[37] Know what you can and can't do, what you are and are not responsible for. Watch your enabling and beware of a high tolerance for inappropriate behavior. These don't do any good. Avoid blunting your feelings and actions with drugs or alcohol. Learn ahead of time how to cooperate and prob-lem-solve with the person with OCD. Have a recovery plan already developed between you and the OCD sufferer. Then, all you have to do is to refer to your plan, or map, and your preparation will give you the principles with which to respond to this individual situation.

Know you will miss some opportunities to practice your new strat-egies. Remember that success is simply getting up one more time than you fall. Remember that the goal in flying through the turbulence of OCD is course correction. You know you will constantly be a little off target and your job is to simply remain headed in the right direction. The goal is to create a longer period of time between incidents and create incidents of shorter duration. The strongest person is the first person to let go of his or her issues when the issues are in the way. Sometimes it will be the person with OCD—after all, he or she is okay when apart from the OCD or when in "OCD-free zones."

Lastly, remember that tears are good: tears are wet and things grow in wetness. Scientific research shows that the kind of secretions con-tained in tears rids the body of unhealthy toxins.

The basic principles in responding versus reacting to the person with OCD allow us to transcend individual situations and create strat-egies that can serve as templates for a wide variety of situations. Hence, the old adage, "Give a person a fish and he will eat today. Teach a per-son to fish and he will eat tomorrow."

No principle is more important than this—There is a space between each stimulus and response. When you learn to appreciate this space and create more of it rather than automatically reacting to your feelings about the situation, you learn to change your responses and, in the process, you change the stimuli.[14] And as icon Virginia Satir, one of the founders of family therapy, said, "If you did nothing more when you have a family together than to make it possible for them to really look at each other, really touch each other, and listen to each other, you would have already swung the pendulum in the direction of a new start."

What Now?

As a creator of your own life within the circumstances that come your way—the hand you've been dealt—you get to choose. No longer are you a part of the small story but a part of something much greater. OCD is still there. It's now about what you do with what's been given you. You have great freedom of choice within these parameters.

Begin to watch for the vibrancy of life. Begin to notice life's beauty and the ecstasy possible despite, or even because of, your special circumstance. Watch for the good stuff. Watch for evidence of your glass being half full, not half empty.

I have said on a number of occasions that getting it together is not about not having any more problems. In some ways, you may actually have more problems because now you are able to successfully juggle more. In this vein I am reminded of a famous quote by Mother Theresa. When asked about her own problems, she said, "I know God will not give me anything I can't handle. I just wish that He didn't trust me so much."

When we get caught up in the drama and chaos of someone else's situation, we become part of the problem. The first stage of dependency and reactivity to the OCD is over. The cat is out of the bag. OCD is understood and accepted and the family is no longer organized in ways that simultaneously disempower it. The next stage in our healing progression ushered in independence and unfolded through the stages of moving beyond the OCD to address your issues. Now you are ready for the last stage of family healing—actually being a healing agent in the family. You are strong enough as an individual to support others in ways you never could before. This is the stage of interdependence.

As a direct result of the period of intense concentration upon the self required by the "Getting It Together" stage, the capacity and ability to be a healing agent for yourself, your family, and loved ones becomes available in ways never experienced before. In the words of psychotherapist Julie Johnson, who has pioneered healing resources for siblings and offspring of the mentally ill, "Hidden victims become hidden healers."

Now that you are caring for yourself, you are more able to attend to the family, including the person with OCD. It is to the healing of the family that we now turn.

—ᗰᗰ—

CHAPTER 7

Healing the Family—From Invisible Survivor to Visible Healer

—〰—

What Is a Family?

You have seen what a family under the influence of OCD is like. It is just as important to know what a family that is not traumatized is like, what a non-traumatized family does, and what makes a family strong. Fortunately, the answers are readily available and easy to learn. Your family is so important that it is never too late to strengthen it.

A family is the group of people to whom you come for nurturance, support, and love and from whom you go forth refreshed, renewed, and ready for the coming day. Your family may be the only place where no one can fill your shoes, the one arena where you are irreplaceable. The most permanent aspect of your life, family is the single most important source of your pain and also your greatest source of pleasure. Some say that to have a family is to ask for trouble. Yet, it is the best investment you might ever make. A family fulfills your basic biological need for belonging.

While rarely a place of short-term comfort, families are around for the long haul of life. You not only begin your life in a family, but, if you're lucky, you end your life in one as well. Your family relationships tend to overflow into all other areas of your life. Have you ever noticed that when everything in the family is right, life is easier? On the other hand, have you noticed that when things in the family aren't going well, life seems harder?

One of the founders of family therapy, psychiatrist Carl Whitaker, said we are all fragments of families. There are no individuals. Poll after public opinion poll, from the Harris to the Gallup poll, consistently show that having a good family life is one of the most important, if not *the* most important, goals in life for the vast majority of people. Perhaps something deep within us realizes the family is the foundation of civilization.

We live in a changing time for the family.[28] No institution has suffered more than the family in the last four decades. Historically, the family has had five major functions: to achieve economic survival; to provide protection; to pass on religious faith; to educate its young; and to confer status. If it met these five major tasks, it was deemed a healthy or strong family. With such simple criteria, it was relatively easy to define a good family: namely, one that was self-sufficient, didn't need help from others, took care of its own, and didn't get into trouble.

Today's family experiences major sociological change. Families aren't needed for economic security. In fact, children are typically a financial drain. For example, it's variously estimated that raising a child to age eighteen now costs somewhere between $200,000 and $400,000. The government may now be the chief protector of families, religious functions have been transferred from the family to the church, and education to the schools, while status has become more a financial issue than the good name or standing of the family within the community.

The functions of the modern family can be summarized by one word: relational. We marry and have children for love, not money. We seek intimacy, not protection. And, as we have seen, it is exactly this function that can be so threatened when OCD strikes a family. The family under the influence of OCD suffers a paradoxical dynamic vis-a-vis dependence: the person who is most dependent is also the most dominant and controlling.

The healthy family is interdependent. The amount of dependence and independence in the family varies according to the ability, age, gender, and education of its members, the amount of external support, and the nature of the circumstances. Dependence has received a bad name recently. Dependence can be healthy, and it changes with your stage of growth, economic freedom, and psychological equilibrium. Regardless, dependency—both healthy and unhealthy—increases when you or a loved one suffers an illness.

What Is a Traumatized Family?

A traumatized family is any family that faces a threat of such magnitude or force that it has the potential to disengage all its positive and protective functions. Those people who are attempting to cope with an extraordinary stressor that has disrupted their normal life in unwanted ways are traumatized.[18] And, as you have discovered, they have similar kinds of problems.

Because the family under the influence of OCD has been traumatized, various members may have different symptoms. All members of the family can be under the spell of OCD but in different ways. They need to learn that their feelings of anguish and terror are normal, even natural, for the situation in which they find themselves. They must learn to be gentle with themselves as they heal.

OCD experts Drs. Jose Yaryura-Tobias and Fugen Neziroglu[62] state that "approximately 50 percent of family members of patients with OCD suffer from some sort of a major psychiatric disorder; in fact, 8 to 10 percent of the parents also suffer from OCD." Yet they also say, "The patient's family is the most important factor during the patient's course of the illness." If you have OCD, it should be clear that it is to your advantage that your loved ones have the opportunity to heal from this illness, too. The more "enrolled" you are in their healing, the more likely they will be enrolled in yours.

What Does Family Healing Mean?

Writing in the 1997 *Journal of the California Alliance for the Mentally Ill,* Donna Mayeux,[14] director of the Louisiana Alliance for the Mentally Ill, reminds us that, "Only when we have developed these essential personal resources of self-renewal [self-care and balance] can we create a more natural and sustainable environment for our mentally ill relative." Reporting on the Journey of Hope program, she adds, "The emphasis on *how we feel* and the emphasis on the importance of *me* and *my well-being* have brought home the important fact that we cannot be of help unless we are in good health physically and mentally."

To be healed is much more than having gotten rid of symptoms or having handled a specific situation correctly.[39] Healing within the family means being a responsible family member and doing your own recovery work. It's no single person's job to heal the entire family. Healing in the family is everyone's responsibility. Taking on this responsibility is heroic and requires time, attention, and effort. Different members of the family have different responsibilities and roles, depending on their age, their place in the family, and the severity of their illness. Parents have different responsibilities than siblings or children, and grandparents have different responsibilities than parents. Even a baby can be healing by its mere presence. The family can develop a healing culture regardless of the behavior of any one member.

If you have OCD, your role can be more muddled because it depends on how many, how often, and what kind of OCD-free time periods you have available. Regardless of your role, however, everyone in the family has their own special responsibilities based on their own unique abilities, skills, and resources. While families develop general rules (for example, "no hitting") that everybody follows, there are also specific rules in the family. For example, based on a behavioral contract developed with a therapist, the person with OCD has ten minutes to lock the doors, mom has Monday nights to go out with her friends, and junior must make his bed each morning.

While egalitarian, the family is not necessarily democratic. Functionality and ability combined with love and awareness determine who has what responsibilities. When those with OCD are deeply entranced by or in the throes of OCD, they temporarily have less responsibility, just as someone who has a fractured knee would not be expected to wash dishes or grocery shop.

When Does Healing Occur?

Family members become well when they have restored their shattered bonds and amended their broken dreams. Only then can family members *safely* maintain a wide variety of healthy, life-enhancing relationships, whether to a mate, friend, religion, career, philosophy, or organization. Healing the family rests upon restoring these connections. The more connections, the stronger the healing.

When we lose connection with ourselves, we become separated from our actions, beliefs, or feelings. We no longer know who we are. No longer knowing what we see, hear, or feel, we are cast adrift in a sea of confusion, doubt, and uncertainty. When we lose connection with others, we forfeit intimacy, the primal joy and awe of sharing with another.

Intimacy is practical! Studies by medical researchers such as cardiologist Dean Ornish show that intimate connections have a measurable impact on physical health. People who feel isolated, for example, have three to five times the mortality rate as those who don't. And when we disconnect from purpose, or vision, we become lost. We lose our spirit. "Without a vision," the Bible states, "the people perish."

At this stage of healing, those who can and who are able to, transition *from* "an individual with individual rights" *to* "an interdependent member of the family." It is necessary for all family members to have rights, limits, and boundaries. What changes is that individuality and rights are placed in context within the family. This allows for intimacy and at the same time provides safety, autonomy, and respect. What is also different now is that you have greater awareness about OCD, more experience with its impact, and a sense of self, especially where one person's needs and feelings begin and where another person's end. Having moved through the initial dependence upon the whims of OCD to a period of independence, it is now possible to come full circle and return to where you started—a devoted member of a family willing to love and be loved, to care and be cared for.

When living in this stage, you are not just a *you*—a parent, spouse, child—but also a family member. Interdependence among family members characterizes this stage. Neither dependent nor independent, family members in this stage of healing are intermingled and interconnected with each other as well as with others outside of the immediate family. Everyone can be appropriately dependent upon others and capable of functioning independently when the situation arises. Throughout the course of all relationships, each person contributes according to his and her ability to participate. Leadership becomes an organizing principle and replaces management. No longer is the primary focus to manage, fix, or muddle through the OCD. In this healing culture, each person has the freedom to be a leader when appropriate. Now the focus is upon strength, initiation, enterprise, choice, and influence.

Different family members have different tasks in healing and treatment. At this stage of healing, if you are an adult family member of an OCD sufferer, you have given up making excuses, believing you are a victim, being reactive, or acting mindlessly. This does not mean that you are perfect, never regress, or slip; rather, your commitment is to "course correct." When you find yourself feeling victimized or reactive, you become aware and shift your attention toward being more proactive. If you are an adult loved one, you're choosing to be accountable to yourself, your family, and other loved ones. Unfortunately, it is not as simple when the OCD sufferer is a child. Nonetheless, as parents you can choose to be accountable to your child in ways you couldn't before.

What Is Necessary for the Family to Begin to Heal?

Paradox and confusion are the two pillars leading to the temple of enlightenment. The family's journey through the five stages of healing is paradoxical and confusing. Initially, the healing may appear linear and separate. In other words, each person becomes aware of the OCD, then identifies core issues, then moves beyond the OCD, then gets it together, and finally becomes a healing agent for the family.

Life is larger, however, than a recovery continuum. Life doesn't move in straight lines. Early in their efforts to deal with OCD, for example, family members may have acted codependently because it seemed necessary. The sufferer needed help and may not have been able to survive without it. However, family members aren't prepared for coping with a chronic, potentially devastating, and hidden disorder like OCD. Poor preparation is hardly the fuel for a long and protracted journey. The family legitimately needs time to assimilate and integrate the OCD experience. It can easily take a year or so to achieve this, and it may be impossible—as well as inadvisable—to prematurely separate or split the family.

Ideally, in the first year of recovery, the five steps actually do work in something like a linear sequence. But somewhere between the first and second year of healing, you become able to be in all stages simultaneously and quickly. By this, I mean you can draw on each of these five different stages—Discovery, Core Issues, Moving Beyond, Getting It Together, and Family Healing—and they become different approaches to the problem, depending on which one is most useful for a particular situation. Because you have choices, you are no longer reactive and are more able to respond in a healthy manner to whatever the situation dictates. In this later healing stage, because you are being a healing agent in the family, you can also work on core issues. Or, as you move beyond, you become aware of some new aspect of the situation in which you are bound and have to get it together and course correct yet another time.

Treatment in the form of psychotherapy, psychoeducational groups, or support groups may be necessary for families so embroiled in core issues that the family members cannot move beyond them. For example, family members may be unable to stop participating in their loved one's compulsions, be depressed, or unable to recognize and act on their own behalf. When members are unable to act, these resources can help them learn to relate to the illness rather than relating from the illness. To accomplish this, the family needs healing agents.

Who Are Family Healing Agents?

Healing agents are people or organizations that serve as a catalyst for change. Anyone can become a family healing agent with work and patience. Becoming one is independent of color, creed, gender, religion, circumstance, or a host of other irrelevant factors. Family healing agents vary in age. The youngest may be in a mother's womb, where the energy of the fetus unites and strengthens the family. A healing agent can be a five-year-old who makes us smile and arouses our protective instincts, or a teenager, adult, or an elder; even the customs, traditions, and rituals we share. Healing agents exist in the form of the institutions that support and empower the family.

Family healing agents are caregivers, not caretakers.[35] When "caretaking," your attempts to rescue, protect, and control others result in self-neglect and a breakdown in relationships. You take care of others, more as a compulsive gesture than as an act of love, freedom, and thoughtfulness. You feel fearful, guilty, insecure, hopeless, lonely, angry, resentful, self-pitying, and full of shame.

Because your boundaries are weak, inappropriate, and permeable, as opposed to clear and firm, you are reactive to others, especially the person with OCD. You find it difficult to initiate or show other signs of leadership. Rather than lead in a situation, you merely manage to get by. You survive and cope rather than flourish and prosper. Your relationships are entangled rather than involved. Finally, the resentment inherent in being a caretaker boomerangs as your anger and frustration are expressed back to you.

When "caregiving," on the other hand, you choose to share yourself. You no longer focus exclusively on the other. You have achieved a vital balance among all your needs. In the process, your concept of giving changes—providing love is a matter of choice and alternatives, not ultimatums. Caregivers understand that sometimes the most you can do for another is set a good example. They know and accept their limitations and respect the power of what they are dealing with.

In the simplest terms, caregivers are those who do the following:

1. Identify their own needs.

2. Ask for what they want.

3. Develop a network of support outside the family.

4. Say "no" when they mean "no."

5. Are true to themselves.

6. Can be loving, nourishing, and respectful.

7. Do all the above on an ongoing basis.

It's very important to know that it is almost impossible to distinguish caretakers from caregivers solely by their behaviors. The behaviors can be identical. But it is where the intentions of the behaviors come from that is important. Are they driven from image and unconsciousness or freedom and mindfulness?

Because caregivers or healing agents have gone through their own dark nights and have faced their own demons, they have the capacity and the space to let the seeds of healing sprout in those they love. Their wounds have become like a crucible for their own excellence,[26] strengthened by the heat of their own pain. To be a family healing agent is to be able to hold many thoughts and feelings without becoming hooked. Healing agents act more like Teflon than Velcro. Little sticks to them, and when it does stick, it comes off easily. They keep returning to their own delicate balance. They know that in order to provide effective care for someone else, they must also understand and care for themselves better.

When Will You Be a Family Healing Agent?

You will be a healing agent for your family whenever you consciously make the choice to be one. Not all or none, black or white, you become a family healing agent anew in each moment of life in which you choose to participate. For some it comes easily, but you can learn to become one by finding other people who are more healed to act as guides.

A family healing agent for the planet, Muhammad Ali has traveled the world preaching unity, love, and spreading God's word despite being stricken with Parkinson's disease. At one point, I wished he had been defeated in the boxing ring because he seemed like an arrogant troublemaker. Now, he is one of my heroes. He has become a living legend. When asked whether he ever gets angry or frustrated because of his disease, Muhammad Ali answered, "It's a blessing." And with his inimical, playful humor, he added, "I always liked to chase the girls. Parkinson's stops all that. Now I might have a chance to go to Heaven."

Though slowed by the physical effects of Parkinson's disease, Ali believes he developed this illness for a reason. In an interview in the January 1997 issue of *People* magazine, wife Lonnie says: "It's not by chance. Parkinson's disease has made him a more spiritual person. Muhammad believes God gave it to him to bring him to another level, to create another destiny."

While I do not believe we cause our illnesses or are responsible for them, I do believe we have a responsibility to find a purpose for them and to recreate anew our life with them. The meaning you give to the OCD provides the fuel for caregiving, whether to yourself or others.

To become a family healing agent is paradoxical. On the one hand, there is nothing you have to do; on the other hand, it requires everything of you. Healing, or what looks like healing, can come from the survival state, which is the domain of the false self. It is fueled by guilt and shame. On the other hand, healing from a place of freedom emanates from the true self and is based on service toward others. It is fueled by love, commitment, and vision. It requires no less than everything we have. It is our journey of a lifetime, our mythic call.

The direction of family healing is toward interconnection and the goal is course correction. Like the pilots of aircraft flying across the skies, the pilot of the mind must expect that there will always be a certain amount of turbulence and bad weather. Your goal therefore isn't a fixed point, rather, it is course correction. Like the pilots who know their direction, but also know they are constantly pushed off course by the wind and weather, you must keep your eye on the donut and not the hole. You must use your energy to reorient toward healing rather than waste it on regrets or on things over which you have no control.

What Contribution Does the Person With OCD Have in Family Healing?

Although the contribution of the OCD sufferer is often missed or overlooked, it should never be underestimated. Those who battle OCD daily and directly are heroes in every sense of the word. As such, they serve as examples of overcoming adversity of the strongest type. Their ongoing struggle should be inspirational to other family members. They also provide opportunities for others to learn and exercise the virtues of patience, compassion, and love. Perhaps most importantly, they remind everyone we all are human, with human frailties. Life is tenuous and unpredictable. "There but for the grace of God go I" is a reminder of how precious life is.

A number of years ago, a woman who had terminal cancer came into one of my psychotherapy groups. She knew she was dying and wanted to be with others who would allow her to have and express her feelings so she could talk about her death. Her gift to her group was an everyday reminder of life's sacredness and brevity. Living with someone who has severe OCD can help us appreciate our good fortune and help us let go of the trivial complaints that clutter our life.

Diane Sands, president of the Obsessive-Compulsive and Spectrum Disorders Association, reminds us that most people with OCD are bright, creative, accomplished, and, at times, highly productive. Most are open, warm, and loving people who want us to know more about them. Sands urges us to ask them, adding that, "It's a relief to talk about our experience in an understanding and non-judgmental environment, and it is critical that you learn."

In sum, the person with OCD has much to offer you and teach you, just as you have much to offer in return. When the love is flowing both ways, healing is available for all.

What Is the Best Healing Family Culture for the Person With OCD?

If, as the great novelist Tolstoy wrote, "All happy families resemble one another; each unhappy family is unhappy in its own fashion," then we should be able to discover those traits that healthy families share in common. Identifying these traits is immensely helpful in supplying us with criteria that we can incorporate, align ourselves with, and emulate. Engaging in these positive, life-enhancing behaviors can strengthen your family because they accomplish one or more of the following:

1. Develop your ability to respond versus react.

2. Encourage reason, not force.

3. Inspire constructive actions.

4. Encourage self-control of emotions, attitudes, and behavior.

5. Emphasize order and organization.

6. Promote mature behavior.

7. Foster love.

8. Make others aware of their impact and the importance of their choices.

9. Acquire the habit of consistency.

Fortunately, there are many researchers who study healthy families through methods like surveys, questionnaires, and interviews. We will look at several of the most important studies in order to discover how, as a healing agent, you can be a model for other family members, how you can mentor and teach, and how you can organize your family activities to help create a positive family culture.

First, in the early 1980s, Dolores Currant, noted columnist, family specialist, and educator, surveyed more than five hundred specialists who work with the family for their insights on "healthy families." She found the following top fifteen behaviors, in order from highest to lowest, were characteristics of the healthy family:

1. Communicates and listens.

2. Affirms and supports one another.

3. Teaches respect for others.

4. Develops a sense of trust.

5. Encourages play and humor.

6. Exhibits a sense of shared responsibility.

7. Teaches a sense of right and wrong.

8. Observes rituals and traditions frequently and regularly.

9. Balances interactions among members.

10. Observes a religious core.

11. Respects the privacy of its members.

12. Values service to others.

13. Fosters family table time and conversation.

14. Shares leisure time.

15. Admits to and seeks help when needed.

Writing from the vantage point of a traumatologist, Charles Figley[18] provides another set of guidelines specifically for the traumatized family. To heal, families must have the following:

1. A clear understanding and acceptance of the stressors affecting them—family members know what they are up against.

2. A family-centered locus of the problem—the focus is shifted from any one family member and recognized as a problem or challenge for the entire family.

3. Solution-oriented problem solving—family members are not stuck in "who is to blame" and move on to mobilize their resources.

4. A high tolerance for one another—family members have even more tolerance for each other during a highly stressful time.

5. Direct expressions of commitment and affections—family members are generous with praise (twenty positive statements occur for each negative one).

6. Open and effective communication—family members not only communicate but the quality and quantity of discussions are higher than those of the average family.

7. High family cohesion—family members enjoy being with each other.

8. Flexible family roles—all members play many roles which depend on the needs of the family, not one member.

9. Efficient resource utilization—the family can access its own resources and ask for help.

10. An absence of violence—effective families, irrespective of the amount of stress and trauma, don't resort to violence; even though highly emotional outbursts occur, from screaming to weeping, they don't end up with violence.

11. Rare substance use—family members don't use drugs as a method of stress reduction.

Nick Stinnett and John DeFrain,[57] two of the most renowned researchers of family strengths, have studied strong families for decades. In studying more than three thousand strong families who responded to questionnaires and interviews, they have summarized a description of strong families. They found that strong families have troubled lives, too, but these families are pleasant, positive places to live because family members have learned beneficial ways to treat each other. They can count on each other for support, love, and loyalty. Members feel good about themselves as a family. They have a sense of belonging with each other, a sense of "we."

Stinnett and DeFrain found six qualities or secrets in strong families:

1. *Commitment.* This is the single most important characteristic. Members are dedicated to promoting each other's welfare and happiness. They value unity and traditions. Members love you for who you are, not for what you do or how they are feeling on a particular day.

2. *Communication.* Family members work at deciphering each other's messages.

3. *Spiritual wellness.* Members have a sense of a greater good or power in life and that belief gives them strength and purpose. It provides meaning, positive outlook, guidelines for living, freedom, and peace.

4. *Time together.* Members spend time together and do it a lot. For strong families the central satisfaction in their lives is the relationship they have with each other.

5. *Appreciation.* Members express many "thank-yous." William James, the father of American psychology, called it the most important need of all.

6. *Coping with crises.* Members view stress as opportunities. To manage stress, they keep things in perspective; humor themselves; take one step at a time; give up worrying; refresh and restore; get outside; exercise; minimize fragmentation; have pets; believe in something bigger than themselves; get a little help from friends; value family and marriage enrichment.

All these qualities are learned. No one family has all or even most of them all the time. Their important message is that strong families are made—step by step—and family members have to work at it constantly. Their effort is ongoing. They continue to work on their relationships. They continue to cherish and nourish the family.

What Should You Do With Your Family Member With OCD in This Stage?

The ideal approach to dealing with your loved ones during their checking, obsessions, or rituals is a proactive one. You and the person with OCD sit down together and decide ahead of time, when everyone's thinking is clear, what the most healing behaviors would be in that particular circumstance. It is critical to have your plan (I often call it the family "vision" when I help a family create the kind of family culture they desire). By having a plan ahead of time that everyone can rely upon, you don't have to decide what to do in the moment. The plan helps label the behaviors (for example, it identifies the OCD and it describes checking), so that you can stop accepting the unacceptable. The plan, not your temporary feelings, determines what behaviors are appropriate. Without a plan, you're more likely to react in old, familiar ways. The plan, of course, must be mutually agreed upon and then you *must stick to it.*

If the OCD sufferer refuses to cooperate, it is nevertheless important to hold the person accountable. This means that the OCD behavior is unacceptable and you may need to apply some gentle but firm pressure to get the person to cooperate. Remember that you can make the horse thirsty. Seeking treatment or some other form of help may be required. It depends on who has the OCD, of course. If it's a child, for example, you can simply require that he or she get treatment. If it's an adult child, you may also be able to require treatment if the person is financially or otherwise dependent upon you. If it's a spouse, you can also require treatment as a condition of marriage, especially if the person is abusive or violent. If it's a friend, you don't have quite as much leverage. But you can be strong in your conviction that your friend needs help. You have to be willing to stand up for what you believe.

At this stage of family healing, one of the most difficult things to do is to leave everybody to their own destiny. This means that no one can always protect another from hurt or injury. Thus, it's not your responsibility to constantly instill calm in the person with OCD. Do the basics: Don't enable. Don't disconnect. Don't participate in rituals. Be loving.

Can You Heal Alone and By Yourself?

Maybe, but why bother? You could also walk to New York from California, but why not take a plane? You'll get there a lot faster and with less wear and tear if you fly. The same idea applies to healing. Instead of an arduous, exhausting trip filled with trial and error or losing your way, your getting support and help facilitates the healing process and maximizes the chances for a positive outcome for everybody.

Getting help amounts to "stacking the deck" in your favor. And in this game of life you need all the help you can get.

What Is Family Therapy?

Family therapy is any treatment administered to one or more members of the family that is designed to promote healing within the family. It's designed to remove the roadblocks to recovery so that the natural process of healing can occur. Family therapy is necessary where there are roadblocks in the way and you can't get them out of the way by yourself.

Family therapy doesn't have to involve the entire family. It can involve one person. But one person in therapy will have an impact on the whole family.

What Are Psychoeducational Groups?

Psychoeducational groups[32] are time-limited approaches to dispensing information and dispelling falsehoods. These groups are designed to provide information about specific illnesses to patients or significant others. The hypotheses underlying these groups is the existence of a biological basis for many chronic illnesses. Attendees are given lectures, shown films, provided literature, and offered opportunities to raise questions in a generally didactic and discussion format.

The goals of these groups are primarily to educate individuals and others about the nature and course of an illness. Hearing specifics about the known biology helps reduce family guilt about "causing" the illness, and efforts are made to educate about the affects of stress on relapse. Treatment alternatives are outlined so that patients and families may make informed choices regarding their options.

Included in these discussions is information about the range of medications, their therapeutic benefits, and side effects. The clinical course of the illness is described, with a goal of clarifying early signs of relapse and the role of early intervention in preventing or delaying increased impairment.

In addition, the dynamics of psychoeducational groups allow participants to identify with one another, decreasing stigmatization and isolation. Knowledge of the course of the illness often alters negative expectations and instills hope. Social linkages made in psychoeducational sessions may be continued outside the meetings, thereby increasing the generally diminished social network of the chronically ill.

Psychoeducational groups are usually limited to six to twelve sessions. More and more centers for the treatment of OCD have instituted family psychoeducational group programs. These allow families of OCD members to meet together on an ongoing basis, with a professional staff member, to learn more about the disorder and how to manage situations in the home.

Is a Spiritual Approach Necessary for Family Healing?

No, it is not essential. Families can recover without a spiritual approach. But while you're dealing with an issue that isn't absolutely necessary for recovery, adopting a spiritual approach clearly makes healing a lot easier. It's like the idea of walking across country or flying mentioned before. You can get there either way, but it sure saves a lot of wear and tear if you fly.

In a wonderful book by Lewis Andrews called *To Thine Own Self Be True,* he provides scientific documentation on the relationship between spiritual values and emotional well-being. It is a particularly helpful book for professional counselors who want to see the "evidence" for spirituality and healing.

Another interesting book edited by William Miller and John Martin called *Behavior Therapy and Religion* reports on a group of behavior therapists who reflect on the integration of behavioral and spiritual approaches to change, including clients' spiritual perspective in cognitive-behavior therapy. Once again, a compelling argument is presented for the value of spirituality in healing.

What Is the Difference Between Leadership in the Family and Managing the Situation?

Leadership is the creation of a healthy family culture that allows all members to grow and develop. Leadership can be defined as "the privilege to have the responsibility to direct the actions of others in carrying out the purposes of the organization, at varying levels of authority, and with accountability for both successful and failed endeavors."

Leadership is based on vision, commitment, love, and strength. Management is based on fear, avoidance, resentment, and intimidation. It is problem-centered. Leadership can bring something new into existence, while management just moves the same old pieces from one place to another. Management is reactive; leadership proactive.

Who Are You Now?

More than a thousand years ago a Chinese Zen master was asked by his student, *"What do you do before enlightenment?"*

"Chop wood and carry water," said the master.

The student then asked, *"What do you do after enlightenment?"*

"Chop wood and carry water," said the master.

You are still the same person and still have the same difficulties as you did when you picked up this book. While you have been reading this book, your circumstances probably haven't changed one bit. Whoever had OCD still has it. The intensity and frequency of the obsessions and compulsions may have shifted, but the actual disorder still remains. I don't know of anyone who talks about "curing" OCD. So, most likely, you will not get rid of OCD. It's a part of the family now.

With the knowledge and skill you have acquired by reading this book, however, you have the greatest opportunity of all—you have the chance to change yourself. And, as difficult as the thought may seem, perhaps you have the opportunity to grow and evolve more than had this trauma not occurred. Thank God! The only possibility you have is the possibility to change yourself. You are the best investment, with the highest yield, that you can make.

The "Big Book" of Obsessive Compulsive Anonymous states, "Living with or being close to someone with OCD can be every bit as difficult as having the problem itself." As we have seen, it doesn't have to be this way anymore. If you follow the steps in this book, you're on the path to family healing. There is much to learn and there is much to do.

You must, however, journey with humility. Please remember the journey can be an arduous one. Perhaps more importantly, it may also be unending. Do not underestimate the influence of the disorder. The influence of OCD is further and wider than many have thought. Its devastation can wreak havoc without notice and upon the strongest of souls.

Your own slips and your own regressions are just an obsession away. But take heart—your own healing can also be a moment away. You might be in the midst of your biggest reaction to the OCD you've had in months. The provocation may even seem slight. The important part is not that you fell under the influence of OCD again—that is inevitable. The important part is that you recognize its pull, discover where your foot is nailed to the floor, move beyond its spell, do what you need to do, and reconnect again. The more you move through this sequence, the more the muscle of your healing ability develops, the more you are healing, the more your family is healing. It's quite simple actually; it's just not at all easy.

Your only task is to course correct as you follow the more marked signposts and pursue those paths that you find and create yourself. Don't waiver. And along the way, be gentle with yourself and others. There are surprises and miracles all along the way.

—ɷ—

CHAPTER 8

Everyday Living—
Practical Answers to Difficult
Questions for Families

—∾—

Why Do You Need to Take Care of Yourself First?

As I have mentioned earlier, your cup can't overflow unless it is full. Therefore, your emotional ship of health must be in good shape before you can deal effectively with the difficult daily circumstances you experience as the loved one of a person with OCD. It is imperative to take time for yourself. Your loved one needs you in his or her life for a long time to come. You must nourish yourself if you are to be available for the long haul.

The thesis of this book is that while it is possible to engage in behaviors that are helpful to the person with OCD, maintaining a healing culture is impossible when you are continually stressed, chronically grief-stricken, forever lonely, and always exhausted. You can sustain healing only when your individual needs are addressed concurrently. Only when your needs are met and maintained will you be able to implement effectively and meaningfully the behavioral, emotional, and spiritual attitudes and skills needed to deal with OCD.

You can burn out doing the right thing when you are doing it for the wrong reasons. When your needs are constantly ignored, denied, and minimized, you have all the ingredients for burnout. Don't burn out. It's not in anyone's best interests if you burn out. Take on your important responsibility to yourself and everyone will benefit.

There are four keys to preventing your burnout. The first key is a good education; you have now obtained this for your key ring. The second key is good self-care. You must assertively put this on your key ring. The third key is effective communication. The fourth is effective action that is consistent with your values, beliefs, and commitments. If you have, in general, followed the principles in this book, you are now ready to add the keys of good communication and effective action.

How Can You Effectively and Meaningfully Interact With the Person With OCD?

First, as has been said over and over in this book, you must address your own needs for healing, love, and support. Without doing this, you will have little stamina for the journey. Next, to relate well to the OCD sufferer, you must be able to separate the person from the illness. You must be able to hear your loved one's voice as louder than the voice of the OCD. You must be able to see your loved one's face as more compelling than the face of the OCD. And your desire for connection with the OCD sufferer must be greater than your wish to disconnect from the OCD. Make sure you are getting comfort and assistance. As long as you are connected to yourself, others, and something greater, you will be getting support and aid.

To remain a healing agent for yourself and those around you, remind yourself often of the essential nature of this illness. When OCD's voice is the loudest, the sufferer is relating to the world from the disorder. The more frequent and the more intense the irrational obsessions, the more severe the illness. OCD gives its sufferers no rest. It can be relentless.

What Do OCD Sufferers Require From Family Members?

What OCD sufferers need most are family members and loved ones who can treat them with dignity, respect, consideration, and love. They need loved ones who can separate the person from the illness—again and again and again. They need loved ones who have learned to break the spell of OCD as well as loved ones who have learned to respond consistently, not react, to the illness. And they need loved ones connected to themselves, others, and something greater.

Loved ones who treat themselves with dignity, respect, consideration, and love are more likely to have mastered the art and science of effective communication and effective action. Communication and action are the foundations upon which relationships are built. They can be broken down into skills and, fortunately, these skills are easily taught and learned, especially when the person (caregiver) is taking good care of himself or herself.

What Basic Principles of Communication Relate to the OCD Sufferer?

All the principles of effective communication can apply to those under the influence of OCD. Rebecca Woolis,[61] for example, in her highly readable book, *When Someone You Love Has a Mental Illness,* presents a repertoire of skills for the family and other caregivers. A number of them can be adapted for dealing with OCD.

The basis from which you can interact effectively is built upon the person with OCD's belief that he or she is understood, taken seriously, and is loved and supported. Without this, there will be no partnership. Give your loved ones the precious gift of accepting them and their illness. The more you understand how your loved ones think and process the world, the more effectively you will be able to interact with them.

The following skills offer methods to do this and lay the foundation upon which you can communicate with your loved one and your loved one can communicate with you. First, communication begins with listening carefully. This means consistently listening to distinguish the voice of OCD from your loved one's voice. Distinguish the person you love, who has his or her special and unique qualities, from the illness. There is a person behind the illness. Speak directly to that person, not the one who is under the spell of OCD. Do not talk to the OCD. When you engage in activities like "checking" for your family member, you are allowing the power of the OCD to increase.

A fine line exists between not engaging in checking or participating in the illness on the one hand, and responding in a humane, loving, and kind manner on the other. Is it a kind deed to support the OCD sufferer in bizarre behavior, like tape recording every conversation, saving every piece of mail, or surfing the web for all the new information on AIDS or the Ebola virus? Or is it kinder to refuse to have your conversations taped, insist that trash mail be discarded, or limit access to the Internet? The former supports the OCD; the latter supports the person who has OCD.

Be calm, clear, and straightforward in all your communications. The environment this creates gives the OCD little to feed upon outside of itself. Do not be afraid to confront sufferers of OCD—that is, to give them feedback on how their behavior is affecting you. State in clear, explicit terms just what the person does. Give descriptions of behavior rather than labels. For example, "You keep following me from room to room demanding that I answer your questions." Say how you feel about it. For example, "I feel violated and angry." Then, state what, if anything, you are requesting. For example, tell the person, "I want to walk around the house without being followed." Use "I" statements instead of giving "you" messages. Tell the person how you feel and what you want and/or need at that moment. Thus, instead of saying, "You are a nuisance," "You are annoying," or "You are a bad person," tell the person, "I get nervous and feel trapped when you ask me the same questions over and over."

When you confront the person with OCD, however, be sure the person is not in the midst of an obvious obsession or compulsion. And don't be surprised if the sufferer has an obsession or compulsion in reaction to your feedback. Anything that increases stress can trigger obsessions and compulsions. Remember, you didn't cause it, you can't control it, you can't cure it, but you can cope with it.

While good communication often makes things better, it is critical to remember that it will not eliminate the OCD sufferer's problems or make him or her well. It's more like air conditioning on a hot day. Effective communication makes the work environment more user-friendly. Remember, too, that communication is a two-way process. Beware of establishing too close a distance with those who are neither in treatment nor recovery. They are exhausting! People with OCD are in recovery when they are accountable, responsible not for the illness, but responsible for managing the illness. This means they get the help and support they need.

Other skills can significantly reduce the amount of frustration and stress you will experience, but will not cure OCD. One is to establish realistic goals. Think small. Pare down expectations. Praise often for each accomplishment, no matter how small, including your own. Take frequent breaks and separate from the OCD sufferer when either of you is upset, which is most likely to be when he or she is in the midst of an obsession and compulsion. Keep what Woolis calls a "loving distance"—that is, the balance between loving and supporting the OCD sufferer on the one hand and not doing for the person what he or she can do for himself or herself on the other. The proverb, "Give a person a fish and he will eat today; teach a person to fish and he will eat tomorrow" applies here.

Another important skill is to set and keep limits, such as you are allowed time alone, you are free to leave the house when you want to and need to, you do not stay around the OCD sufferer when you feel abused, or you are not required to shower before entering the house. Know your limits. Establish your boundaries. Be clear about what is your boundary and what is another person's boundary. Make rules that protect everybody, rules such as no checking or not doing for another what that person can do for himself or herself. Know that some days you won't have the clarity or strength to be a healing agent. Learn to recognize the agitation of loved ones, and always allow them a graceful exit. Most importantly, don't take the negative words or actions of the OCD sufferer personally, and certainly don't argue with the person when he or she is in the midst of the OCD.

Continue to maintain a positive attitude. You do have control over yourself even though you don't have control over the OCD. Educate yourself on an ongoing basis since information about OCD is changing daily, and be sure to talk with supportive people.

Remember, too, that family members may need a trained professional to help them initiate these skills. OCD sufferers can be angry and difficult if loved ones try to withdraw their participation in rituals.

How Do You Respond to the OCD Sufferer When He/She Is in the Midst of an Obsession or Compulsion?

I have already addressed an aspect of this question in a previous chapter by suggesting that the family, together with the OCD sufferer, create a clear, concrete plan or vision of how they will respond to an OCD attack. For example, having a plan predetermines that when the OCD sufferer is so entranced by the OCD that he or she is intrusive and is violating your boundaries or exceeding your limits, you go to your room, the sufferer goes to his or her room, or some other concrete steps are implemented. Then, when the violation occurs and you verbalize this, everyone complies with the predetermined plan. This minimizes chaos and confusion and allows for a cooling-off period.

It is not uncommon that a therapist may be needed to mediate in this planning. There will be times when the OCD sufferer finds it difficult or impossible to follow the plan and stay with the vision. When this happens, first avoid any attempts to reason the person out of the OCD. Additionally, avoid reassuring the person out of the OCD, attempting to argue the person out of the OCD, or intimidating or shaming the person out of the OCD. All of these strategies will backfire and make the OCD worse. Your job is to keep to your part of the plan.

If the person with OCD is so persistent with questions or statements that he or she is in your face, take a deep breath and first get clear while bringing all of your focus and clarity to the current difficulty. Remember all that you have learned about OCD. OCD casts its doubt on all of us. Then, say something like, "I find this unpleasant and I need to separate from you now." Or, "I can't answer your question.

I love you and answering your question could make the OCD worse." Most importantly, do not debate who's right. Be calm, clear, centered; don't belittle, don't mock, don't make fun of, don't enter lengthy discussions about the content, and don't escalate the situation by allowing your anger to hook you. If you are having difficulty managing your anger, get more physical distance until you calm down.

Keep surrendering to the fact that the incessant questions are about the illness, not the person. Lead the conversation away from the topic of the obsessions or rituals and clearly and without judgment express your desire to change the subject. If it seems appropriate, knowing the person as you do, offer the OCD sufferer help in coping with the feelings. For example, you could ask, "What can you or I do to help right now that is outside of the OCD?" Of course, if this were to feed the OCD, it would be an inappropriate question.

How Involved Should You Be in Your Loved One's Life?

This issue addresses such thorny questions as, "How much should I help?" and "Why shouldn't I do everything to make it easier for my loved one?" These are never easy questions to answer, because they depend on the person who has the OCD, how severe the OCD is, how old the parties are, and a host of other conditions. No single answer applies to all situations.

Your answers are closely related to your evaluation of realistic goals and expectations. Your answers must also be influenced by the variable nature of the illness. Since OCD symptoms are cyclical, you must be prepared to change with them. Keep a loving distance. Also, your answers depend on the person's willingness to follow your advice, the amount of influence and leverage you have with the person, or whether or not there is a legal relationship present.

You know that loved ones are overprotected if they look to you or others to do things for them before trying to do the things themselves. Also, if your loved ones consistently back away from taking any small step toward increased responsibility and independence, it is likely they are being overprotected.

Always do all you can to protect the sufferer from clear and present danger to self or others. Contact police or other emergency services if someone's life is at risk.

How Do You Deal With Your Loved One's Abusive Behavior?

Abuse can be defined in many ways, but it generally encompasses treating someone like an object. Abuse can be subtle. One of the most common forms of abuse in families under the influence of OCD is for OCD sufferers to involve family members or friends in their obsessions and compulsions. Thus, in some families, members are literally required to take off their clothes and scrub themselves down before entering the home, while members in other families might be forced to rent more space to accommodate all the "stuff" that their hoarding relative has accumulated. Another common form of abuse occurs when the OCD sufferer either gets excessively angry and aggressive or ignores and withdraws from you when you refuse to participate with the OCD.

Family members enable the abusive behavior when they allow it to occur unchallenged. As Eldridge Cleaver once said, "If you're not part of the solution, you're part of the problem." While you have the right to not like the abusive behavior and are entitled to feel hurt and angry, it doesn't pay to linger with the pain. Rather, you have the responsibility to deal with your feelings, too—lovingly and tenderly. Then, firmly convey to the offending party what his or her behavior is, how you feel about it, and what you are requesting (remember, be clear and specific and choose one behavior).

Abuse, however, is a two-way street. Not only can you be abused but you can be an abuser. When you yell and scream or give your loved one the silent treatment, you are being abusive. When you also keep the sufferer dependent on you because you do everything for them, you are being abusive. While your abuse doesn't cause the OCD and being non-abusive won't cure it, an atmosphere free of abuse creates a healing culture in which everyone's quality of life is increased.

How Do You Deal With Your Loved One's Anger?

Inappropriate management of anger is one of the major ways in which abuse occurs. It is easy to become frightened or aggressive yourself in the face of another's anger. Your family member's anger can come in two forms. It is important to be able to distinguish between the two.

The first type of anger is appropriately taken personally, because it is about you. You have committed some transgression, or you have violated your loved one's space. For example, you keep interrupting and speaking for your partner, you ridicule and make fun of your loved one, or you act in an untrustworthy way by undercutting his or her progress. In these cases, you need to acknowledge your behavior or mistakes, apologize, and agree to stop the offending behavior. Remember that anger is rarely a primary feeling. This means that most times there is another emotion, often fear or hurt, underneath the anger. Address these underlying feelings with your loved one. When you deal with your thoughts and feeling in these ways, you are modeling being responsible for your loved one, and in the process your are acting heroically in the mythic sense. Be a hero to someone in your family in this way.

The second form in which your loved one's anger can arise relates more to the OCD than you. This anger is not personal; it is not about you, although you are personally affected. In fact, expect the OCD sufferer's anger whenever you are in the way of the OCD. For example, if you refuse to participate in checking, or you offer information contrary to the OCD, or if you refuse to listen to the endless ramblings of the OCD (in other words, act like a hero in the mythic sense), you may be the recipient of a blast of anger.

In the latter situations, where OCD is in control of your loved one, it is critical that you don't get hooked by the anger, or OCD's manifestations. Be proactive, rather than reactive, and anticipate anger in those situations. Put your planned response to inappropriate anger into action. Forewarned is forearmed!

There are also ways to communicate that will defuse the anger. But to be able to use them, you must be in control of yourself. If both of you are angry and upset, it is best to separate until at least *you* calm down. From this calm state, talk slowly and clearly. Stay in control of yourself. Avoid provoking the person by challenging or not giving the person a way out. Avoid touching the person without permission. Either communicate a sense of assurance or tell the person you are frightened by his or her behavior and to please stop. If the behavior doesn't stop, leave the room. Curb arguing with your loved one. Allow the person a graceful way out; don't back the person against a wall with "either-or" statements. Acknowledge the person's feelings and demonstrate that you are willing to understand what the person is experiencing. Help the person decide what to do next to reduce the anxiety or upset. Protect yourself and others from injury. Advance preparation for these situations is your greatest asset.

Most importantly, when you do get hooked—which you will—get off the hook quickly. The quicker you are off the hook, the quicker you take the person with OCD off the hook and the less reactive and responsive to the OCD he or she will be. Expect that sometimes you will get hooked by the OCD.

If your loved one's anger is recurring, have a crisis plan ready, keep emergency phone numbers and procedures in a convenient place, know your limits, and know how you will proceed when they are exceeded. Tell your loved one what you will do when these limits are exceeded. Tell the person, for example, "You must not yell and scream. If you do, I will leave."

Finally, use the energy your anger contains to do something meaningful for yourself and others. Many of the early pioneers on the impact of mental illness upon the family had ill family members themselves. Their pain became a crucible for their own growth and healing. Your anger can also help you build a career, get a promotion, develop a hobby, or get into an exercise program if you tap into the energies it embodies.

How Do You Deal With the OCD Sufferer When Violence Is an Issue?

While violence is seldom or rarely a problem in families under the influence of OCD, it occurs more frequently in families of all kinds—and the families of OCD sufferers are no exception. Some family members may fear homicide or physical injury. Also, some fear their relative will act out aggressive obsessions. Cooper notes in her study of OCD's effects on the family, that while children are usually not violent themselves, acts of violence are not uncommon among teenagers with OCD. The result can be parents who often "walk on egg shells." What is most common is that some sufferers will be angry and abusive rather than violent when they are interrupted during an obsession or compulsion.

Regardless, the first rule about violence in the family must be that violence is unacceptable. In fact, it is grounds for requiring the offending person to leave the house either temporarily or permanently. Violence is a "deal breaker"—that is, if the person engages in violence, the deal of direct support and caring is over.

One of best indicators of whether an individual has the potential to be violent is the person's past history. If the person has never been violent, he or she is unlikely to be so in the future. If violence has occurred, examine the circumstances to determine if it might happen again. Was the person in the midst of an obsession or compulsion, intoxicated, off medication, or is there another untreated psychiatric illness present in addition to the OCD?

The key to handling violence is prevention. Violence usually has a distinguishable beginning, middle, and end phase. Study your situation and see where you can intervene in this process. If you can't stop or alter the process, this is important information. In all cases your safety and the safety of family members must be protected first. Remove yourself from the situation if you believe that you are in danger.

How Do You Deal With Suicide and Its Wake?

Suicide is one of the most feared and least discussed aspects of OCD. People with OCD commit suicide. As Cooper notes in her study of family members, "The report of suicidal behavior by 12 percent of OCD relatives conforms to statistics on suicide among depressed persons in the general population." Furthermore, a great many more people with OCD contemplate suicide, obsess over it, or fight daily with these thoughts. OCD is a torturous illness when the person is not in recovery or when the sufferer is not responding to treatment. OCD inflicts suffering of the worst kind—a sense of helplessness and hopelessness.

Consequently, many families live in constant dread that their loved one may resort to suicide, whether because of relentless obsessive doubt, a need to end suffering, or a desire to stop being a burden to the family. Sometimes other family members are asked to assist in committing suicide. While it is easy to judge OCD sufferers for dwelling on death or even wanting to die, it is impossible for us to know how we might react if, in fact, we were in the same situation, suffering as they are suffering.

Fortunately, there are often warning signs before someone attempts suicide. If your loved one is feeling extremely worthless, utterly hopeless, or shows a sudden shift in mood from severe depression to inexplicable brightness or serenity, puts his or her affairs in order, has had previous suicide attempts, and has a concrete plan, including the ways and means, then the probability of an attempt—and success—is higher. Indeed, the more of the above conditions that are present in one person, the higher the probability that suicide will be a possibility.

There are relatively simple yet powerful preventative measures that decrease the likelihood of suicide. You can use them whether you are being helped by a professional or not. (And if suicide is an issue, it would be a good idea to involve a skilled professional.) Take seriously any talk or conversation of suicide by the person with OCD—or any family member for that matter. The person may be reaching out to you.

Do not ignore or minimize; empathize. For example, say, "It must be terrible to feel that way." Or, "I bet you are really scared when you look at situations that way." Offer support and encouragement. Educate the OCD sufferer. Let the person know how common thoughts of death and suicide can be and that they can pass if he or she is patient.

Suicidal thinking is generally an acute problem, although there are some families in which suicide seems to permeate the generations. Encourage the sufferer to seek professional help. Make a written contract with the person in which he or she promises not to commit suicide without talking to you first.

Sometimes, even when everyone does all the right things at the right time, people manage to kill themselves with no warning. Nothing anyone can do will prevent them from doing this. A little-known statistic reveals that more suicides occur in hospitals than at home. When someone is intent upon killing himself or herself, there is little that can be done. And when this happens, everyone around the victim feels responsible. Every relative, friend, and professional involved thinks he or she could have prevented the death by doing one or two more things. More often than not, however, no one could have prevented it.

If your relative or loved one is contemplating suicide, or if a family member recently committed suicide, *get help immediately.* Hesitation can be deadly. Further, the probability of a devastating outcome is exaggerated when you try to deal with situations like this alone.

Let us not forget that family members of those with OCD also commit suicide. They, too, sometimes live under constant or chronic stress. They, too, can feel that life is too difficult and too full of despair.

What Do You Do if a Loved One Has a Substance Abuse Problem in Addition to OCD?

There is a very simple model that can be used to tell if someone has an addiction or substance abuse problem, which I describe in *Recovery: A Guide for Adult Children of Alcoholics.* It is "use-trouble-use." In other words, if someone uses a drug, substance, or activity, and *gets into some kind of trouble* (for example, gets arrested for drinking and driving, fired from a job because of drinking, makes poor financial decisions, or hurts someone when drunk), then uses that same drug, substance, or activity again, and does this repeatedly, then that person is addicted.

Substance abuse and addiction are fueled by trauma, secrecy, denial, abandonment, shame, and loss of self.[26] All of these ingredients are present in the majority of families under the influence of OCD. I believe we are witnessing a rise in addiction in all illnesses and among all kinds of families. Also, more often than we may want to realize, family members become dependent upon anti-anxiety agents and sleeping pills.

If your loved ones with OCD are dependent upon alcohol or other drugs at the same time, they have what mental health practitioners call a "dual diagnosis." They will not only have all of the problems associated with OCD but all of the problems associated with chemical dependency—denial, minimization, rationalization, and a general and progressive distortion of reality.

When a loved one is chemically dependent, the chemical dependency becomes the primary problem—the one that must be treated first. If it is not treated, it will limit the recovery from OCD. The substance abuse will always make OCD worse in the long run—not only for the primary sufferer but for the family as well.

Family members can help in a variety of ways. First, members must talk about the problem. Each must express his or her concerns openly and honestly. Denial must be overcome. Encouraging the OCD sufferer to accept the dependence problem is the first and often most difficult step. Seek professional help. Then encourage the sufferer to attend support groups like Alcoholics Anonymous, and you should explore the possibility of participating in Al-Anon or other support groups for families. Neither OCD nor substance abuse will disappear if ignored. Both are serious and can be life-threatening. You must face them directly and learn how to deal with both. It would be wise to get professional help from someone who knows both OCD and chemical dependency.

How Do You Deal With Your Loved One's Bizarre Behavior?

Once again, you, the family hero, are being asked to deal with the fact that your loved one has a major problem. In a mythical sense, the king and queen of the realm are under siege and a hero is needed to champion the order. Knights are needed to defend the realm or an ordinary person is singled out and must find the Holy Grail—in this case the dragon is a neurobiological disorder, and the challenges and "trials" through which you must pass are the symptoms associated with this illness.

The OCD behavior can be so out of the range of ordinary experience (a definition of trauma) that it appears bizarre to us—and to others, as well—but not necessarily to the person with OCD. There is no invisible shield which protects you from it. It takes only a moment's thought to remember that your loved one is lost in an obsession or crippled by a compulsion.

So, once again, the task is to take a deep breath—literally take a breath—and decide how to avoid surrendering (not succumbing or submitting) to the fact that your loved one has OCD. Do this again and again, until surrender's muscle is so strong that you have the spaciousness, or capacity, to "be with" exactly what is happening and exactly what is not happening. In these moments of time, you are off the hook of blame and shame, feelings which "lock" you into physical, emotional, or spiritual deficit. In the ongoing surrender to your inability to control the OCD comes your freedom.

Remember the basics about the bizarre behavior: it is a symptom of the OCD, you didn't cause it, you can't control it, it usually doesn't require a response from you, and you can cope with it. Decide what your limits are regarding the behavior and share them with the parties involved when you are calm and clear. Decide in advance what consequences there will be; follow through with them; and then move on and shift the focus.

How you respond to the bizarre behavior depends on a number of conditions. The first to consider is the likelihood and degree of danger to the OCD sufferer and to others. If the bizarre behavior poses a real danger—for example, your loved one getting out of the car on a busy freeway—do everything you can to preserve his or her safety as well as others. Recognize, however, that in a number of situations, including those with the potential for danger, you may not be able to stop the person, but you can advise your loved one that you believe what they intend is dangerous and will lead to harm—harm to themselves or to others.

When the behaviors are harmless, it is best to ignore them. In other words, pick your battles carefully. If the person's behaviors are embarrassing or disturbing to you, you may ask your relative to refrain from engaging in them while in your presence or while in a public place. Keep in mind the basic communication skills for dealing with your loved one in situations such as these: describe the behavior clearly and without judgment, describe how you feel, and state all requests in clear "I" messages.

Why Are Vacations and Holidays So Difficult When It Would Appear That They Are Occasions to Celebrate and Enjoy?

Sometimes, OCD individuals do well on vacations. Out of their daily routine, they take a vacation from the illness. Nevertheless, holidays, and to a lesser degree vacations, are difficult for many people, including people who do not have OCD. Many people are so cut off from themselves and so dependent upon their work or familiar surroundings that they become anxious and depressed when they don't have anything to do or when they are in strange places. Holidays can be very difficult for many distressed people. They remind them of times long ago, of their lost dreams, and of unfulfilled expectations, all of which fuel stress because of the additional stimulation as well as pressure. Holidays often accentuate the feelings of "being different" because distressed people find it so difficult to relate to others through the filter of their illness.

For the OCD sufferer in particular, however, vacations and holidays are often one long, protracted, and unrelenting exposure trial. On holidays and vacations, OCD sufferers are exposed to new situations continuously. In fact, these occasions involve exposure after exposure. Thus, it would be quite naive—as well as foolish—to expect the OCD sufferer to have a good time on either occasion.

Many fights can be avoided when you realize this one simple truth: vacations and holidays are not fun for a great many OCD sufferers, particularly those who are not in treatment or recovery. Under the best of circumstances, they are challenges even to those in middle and late recovery from OCD.

Should Your Loved One Live at Home When the OCD Is Severe?

This question is asked most often by parents who wonder how long an adult child should continue to live with them. As with other questions, there are no hard and fast rules. Each situation is different. Regardless, the heart of the decision is the well-being of the person with OCD weighed against the well-being of other family members. While no family member wishes to see the OCD sufferer impoverished or "out on the street," the impact on everybody of taking the distressed member into the home can be enormous and shouldn't be undertaken lightly.

The consensus among both experienced family members and professionals[29,30,41,42,61] is that once the family member is old enough and independent enough, everyone seems happier when the sufferer lives away from home and enjoys regular contact with the family and receives necessary support. The person with OCD seems to function at a higher level and the family is less taxed.

A number of conditions need to be in place, however, to favor a positive outcome or experience when the OCD sufferer still lives at home. They include some of the following: the sufferer's symptoms don't disrupt the overall functioning of the family on a consistent basis; the person has a social life, including at least one friend to depend upon outside the family; no siblings live at home; the sufferer is in treatment, whether medication, therapy, or OCA; there is a strong parental team; family members have influence and leverage over the sufferer; and last, but not least, the family undergoes a family-skills training program such as offered by Journey of Hope.

How Can You Make Effective Decisions?

There are a number of excellent models for making decisions work. They are helpful whether the individual with OCD participates or not. And while they are easy to describe, they are more difficult to implement because you must exercise commitment, intention, and action. When you implement some or all of the following eight steps, you can help yourself and your family create effective solutions to many daily problems.

1. Call a family meeting and have as many people as possible attend.

2. Have each person clearly define the problem as he or she experiences it, being sure to listen to everybody, including the person with OCD. Always speak to the person and acknowledge the OCD.

3. Write down all of the problems. There is something about putting them on paper that helps get a better handle on them.

4. Brainstorm with everybody present all possible solutions to the problem. Don't evaluate whether or not the proposed solutions are realistic at this point.

5. Discuss the pros and cons for each proposed solution.

6. Choose the best solution.

7. Implement the solution through a clear step-by-step procedure.

8. Evaluate the effectiveness of the solution and course correct when necessary. This simple procedure goes a long way to reduce conflict among family members and maintain a healing culture.

How Do You Deal Effectively With the Mental Health System?

Your loved one will probably require some kind of intervention—and likely, it will involve more than one mental health professional, especially if the person's OCD becomes severe. It is important for you to know how to interface with the mental health system and to become an active member of the therapeutic team.

To play effectively on the team, you must learn the rules of the mental health system. First, the rules pertain to whoever has the power and influence. There are different rules that depend upon whether your loved one can live independently or whether he or she needs some sort of residential treatment. In the former, a psychiatrist—a physician by training—is typically the lead player, while in the latter, a case manager might be the most important player.

A good rule is to learn the cast of characters. The team could be composed of a psychiatrist for medication, a behavioral therapist for the exposure and response prevention, a psychologist or social worker for the family, and a case manager or conservator if the person is that disturbed.

Another critical rule is to treat the various members of the team just as you want them to treat you. The Golden Rule applies here as well as it does everywhere else. Ask for what you want and tell the various members what you need. Be proactive rather than reactive with your team. Anticipate the roadblocks ahead. Plan for them actively. Learn to live with *your* fear and develop a relationship with it. Don't live from it.

Probably the single most important consideration in choosing a team member is that the person has experience with the specific kind of illness with which you and your relative are suffering. Remember, too, that any team member is fallible and can make mistakes. Trust your own intuition and do not be afraid to get a second opinion or even fire a team member who is not doing his or her job well. Not all health providers are skilled in treating OCD and its wake.

What Can You Do When Your Loved One Refuses Treatment?

This is a tricky issue because it often depends on the age and your relationship with your loved one. Perhaps it is easiest when the person is a child or even an adolescent. In these situations, you have a great deal of control. It can be the most difficult when the loved one is a parent. Spouses and siblings seem to fall in the middle. Nonetheless, you may have more leverage than you think.

Remember the adage, "You can lead a horse to water, but you can't make the horse drink." Well, that is true, but it is also true that you can make the horse thirsty. And one of the best ways to make the person with OCD "thirsty" is to know WHY the person is refusing treatment.

Probably the most common reasons are fear and ignorance. Treatment involves change, and OCD sufferers typically abhor change. The prescription for well-being literally exposes the sufferer to his or her worst fears. Thus, if the person fears contamination, treatment involves exposing the person to the possibility of germs and illness. Many sufferers also fear anti-depressants will somehow injure or harm them and overlook the potential benefits of medications. Providing sufferers with clear and accurate information as well as education can be the first step in enrolling them in treatment. Explaining what will and will not happen can be just the stimulus to seek the aid that sufferers need.

Denial of the illness prevents many sufferers from getting the help they need. Behaviors that enable sufferers to avoid the consequences of their behaviors fuel denial. To break their denial and to accept their condition exposes sufferers to a host of losses as well as new responsibilities. It can be easier to remain ill. Helping the person accept the diagnosis, therefore, increases his or her likelihood of entering treatment. We are not moved to do something about which we are unaware.

Secondary gain, or the benefit one gets from being ill, also prevents some sufferers from receiving the help they need. They have learned to avoid responsibility by being ill and have received a great deal of attention from being unable to engage in normal activities. Thus, some sufferers are reluctant to give up their disorder because they believe they will not be able to replace the attention they are used to. In such situations, it is critical to help the person discover more positive ways to get attention.

Regardless of the reason, the key to making those who resist treatment "thirsty" is to discern the reason or reasons that prevent them from receiving the help they need and then "to speak" to the reasons. Sometimes, too, the only thing that will cause some sufferers to go into treatment is giving them a deal they can't refuse. In other words, if they are to continue to receive your help and support, they simply must get help. While such "requests" may seem hard, tough, or even cruel, they are sometimes the only choice. Tough love is as applicable to those with OCD as it is to those who suffer substance abuse problems and other problems of irresponsibility. It is said that active alcoholics don't have relationships; they only take hostages. The same can be said of OCD sufferers who will not enter treatment. It can be impossible to deal with someone who has OCD and refuses appropriate treatment.

And finally, remember that there are times when there is absolutely nothing you—or anyone else—can do to make your loved one enter treatment. I often tell my clients that one of the most difficult road-blocks to their recovery is their inability to leave their loved ones to their own fate.

What About the Future?

In all recorded history, the future has never been brighter for those under the influence of OCD—from the OCD sufferer to family members and significant others. Advances in medicine are resulting in more and more powerful drugs, with fewer and fewer side effects. New medications and therapeutic discoveries are occurring every year—and in some cases, every month. Anything can become possible in this climate, including a cure for OCD, whether the cure is biological, psychological, spiritual, or, more likely, a combination of all three.

In addition, there is a growing family-based movement where families are getting the education, support, and practical skills they need from outside the traditional mental health field. OCA and the Journey of Hope are two prime examples of family-based healing. Organizations like the OC Foundation, the OC Information Center, or NAMI (the National Alliance for the Mentally Ill), provide leadership and direction through the darkness of OCD. Further, there are now a host of books, documentaries, journals, Internet Websites, and television shows that are bringing OCD out of the shadows.

Poised in history, straddling the line between danger and opportunity, you face a unique series of choices. If you accept the challenge and confront OCD for what it is, an aberrant, mutant brain disorder that gives its sufferers false experiences appearing real (FEAR), and if you accept the traumatic impact those under its influence can experience, then all of us can join together and be strong enough to break its spell.

If you do your work, your children and your families will have less trauma. And if your children and their children have less to deal with, then your grandchildren will have less to deal with and you will have passed onto them a legacy of hope and possibility and vision.

And in the process, you will have played your hand well indeed. Congratulations!

—⚬⚬⚬—

A Final Note to Families —from Robin

—⚉—

In reviewing the literature on OCD and the family, I came across this note "From Robin" that appeared in an early OC Foundation newsletter. She immediately touched my heart with her words, and I am honored to share her list of what she would tell her loved ones. Her words are just as relevant and cogent today as they were when she wrote them in 1989.

If I could tell my family and close friends what I would like them to know about OCD and what it is like for me, I would tell them some of the following things I have listed:

- First, I did not choose this disorder. I did not choose this any more than people choose to have epilepsy, diabetes or allergies.

- The disorder is nasty, intrusive, and sometimes embarrassing to me, and I get no pleasure in having it.

- Try to direct your anger at the disorder, instead of only being angry at me. I hate the disorder more than you do because I have to fight it every single day.

159

- Please notice my gains in fighting this disorder. Fighting OCD requires a great deal of work and personal courage. Please find a way to appreciate my struggle, though you may not understand it.

- Be informed. Read about the disorder. Research in OCD is in an exciting state. New information about it is increasing. The more we know about this problem the better we can fight this thing. Becoming a member of the OCD Foundation is a good way to accomplish this goal. Its newsletters and mailings will keep you informed about the latest advances in the fight against OCD.

- If I go to an OCD support group, please join me from time to time. Allow me to be helpful to you. No matter how bad I feel, I still want to be able to give something to you.

- Be a supporter instead of an enabler.

- Think of what I can do, instead of what I cannot do.

- Please try to think of me as a full person. The OCD is only part of what I am. Think of me as having the Obsessive-Compulsive disorder, not as me being the Obsessive-Compulsive disorder.

- A kind word goes a long way.

(From the OCD Newsletter, 1989)

—m—

APPENDIX A

Where to Get More Help

—ᗰᖫ—

**The Awareness Foundation for OCD &
Related Disorders (AFOCD)**
564 Cuesta Drive
Aptos, CA 95003
Telephone: (831) 684-9684
E-mail: jamescallner@sbcglobal.net
Website: www.ocdawareness.com

Anxiety Disorders Association of America (ADAA)
8730 Georgia Avenue, Suite 600
Silver Spring, MD 20910
Telephone: (240) 485-1001
Fax: (240) 485-1035
Website: www.adaa.org

Child Psychopharmacology Information Service (CPIS)
UW-Madison, Wis. P.I.C.
6001 Research Park Boulevard, #1568
Madison, WI 53719-1179
Telephone: (608) 263-6171
Website: www.library.wisc.edu/libraries/childpharm.htm

Federation for Children With Special Needs (FCSN)
1135 Tremont Street, Suite 420
Boston, MA 02120
Telephone: (617) 236-7210
Fax: (617) 572-2094
E-mail: fcsninfo@fcsn.org
Website: www.fcsn.org

Journey of Hope
(NAMI Louisiana)
11762 South Harrell's Ferry Road, Suite D
Baton Rouge, LA 70816
Telephone: (225) 292-6928
Fax: (225) 368-0055
Website: http: la.nami.org/programs.html

The Journal
California Alliance for the Mentally Ill
1111 Howe Avenue, Suite 475
Sacramento, CA 95825
Telephone: (916) 567-0163
Website: www.healthieryou.com/journal.html

National Alliance for the Mentally Ill (NAMI)
Colonial Place Three
2107 Wilson Boulevard, Suite 300
Arlington, VA 22201-3042
Telephone: (703) 524-7600
Info Helpline: (800) 950-6264
Fax: (703) 524-9094
TDD: (703) 516-7227
Website: www.nami.org

National Institute of Mental Health (NIMH)
Office of Communications
6001 Executive Boulevard, Room 8184 MSC 9663
Bethesda, MD 20892-9663
Telephone: (301) 443-4513; toll-free: (866) 615-6464
Fax: (301) 443-4279; fax-on-demand: (301) 443-5158
TYY: (301) 443-8431
E-mail: nimhinfo@nih.gov
Website: www.nimh.nih.gov

National Organization for Rare Disorders (NORD)
55 Kenosia Avenue
Post Office Box 1968
Danbury, CT 06813-1968
Telephone: (203) 744-0100; Voice mail: (800) 999-6673
Fax: (203) 798-2291; TDD: (203) 797-9590
E-mail: orphan@rarediseases.org
Website: www.nord-rdb.com

Obsessive-Compulsive Anonymous
Post Office Box 215
New Hyde Park, NY 11040
Telephone: (516) 739-0662
Website: www.hometown.aol.com/west24th/index/html

Obsessive-Compulsive Foundation, Inc. (OCF)
676 State Street, New Haven, CT 06511
P.O. Box 9573, New Haven, CT 06535
Telephone: (203) 401-2070
Fax: (203) 401-2076
E-mail: info@ocfoundation.org
Website: www.ocfoundation.org

Obsessive-Compulsive Information Center (OCIC)
Madison Institute of Medicine
7617 Mineral Point Road, Suite 300
Madison, WI 53717
Telephone: (608) 827-2470
Fax: (608) 827-2479
E-mail: mim@miminc.org
Website: www.miminc.org/aboutocic.html

OCD Online
Website: www.ocdonline.com

Peace of Mind Foundation, Inc.
1200 Wilcreast Drive
Houston, TX 77042
Telephone: (281) 960-8855
E-mail: emcingvale@hotmail.com
Website: www.peaceofmind.com

Tourette Syndrome Association, Inc. (TSA)
42-40 Bell Boulevard
Bayside, NY 11361-2820
Telephone: (718) 224-2999; toll-free (888) 486-8738
Website: www.tsa-usa.org

Trichotillomania Learning Center
303 Potrero Street, Suite 51
Santa Cruz, CA 95060
Telephone: (831) 457-1004
Fax: (831) 426-4383
E-mail: info@trich.org
Website: www.trich.org

Well Spouse Foundation
63 West Main St., Suite H
Freehold, NJ 07728
Telephone: (800) 838-0879
Website: www.wellspouse.org

APPENDIX B

Recommended Reading

—〰—

Chansky, T. *Freeing Your Child From Obsessive-Compulsive Disorder: A Powerful, Practical Program for Parents of Children and Adolescents.* New York: Three Rivers Press, 2001.
An excellent resource for parents by a highly skilled clinician.

Foa, E. and Wilson, R. *Stop Obsessing!* New York: Bantam, 1991.
A sound book on exposure and response prevention by two leading pioneers and authorities on OCD.

Fitzgibbons, L. *Helping Your Child With OCD: A Workbook for Parents of Children With Obsessive-Compulsive Disorder.* Oakland: New Harbinger Publications, 2003.
This parent-friendly workbook provides assessments, fill-ins and progress charts that encourage parents to be involved and stay committed to their child's recovery from OCD.

Gravitz, H. L. and Bowden, J. D. *Recovery: A Guide for Adult Children of Alcoholics.* New York: Simon and Schuster, 1987.
A classic on the impact of alcoholism on the family—more than 400,000 copies in print.

Greist, J. H. *Obsessive-Compulsive Disorder: A Guide,* rev. ed. Obsessive-Compulsive Information Center, Dean Foundation, Madison, WI, 1997.
An information-loaded guide for people with OCD, their families, friends, and interested others. It is one of the best places to start your journey of information and education.

Jenike, M., Baer, L., and Minichiello, W. *Obsessive-Compulsive Disorder: Theory and Management,* 2nd ed. St. Louis: Mosley Year Book, 1990.
A single, comprehensive, and thoroughly annotated reference book covering virtually every aspect of OCD. It is for the advanced reader.

Landsman, K. *Loving Someone With OCD: Help for You & Your Family.*
Oakland: New Harbinger Publications, 2005.
Written for partners of those who suffer with obsessive-compulsive disorder, this book offers a step-by-step program to assist their loved ones with activities like ritual prevention, exposure techniques, as well as stress and anxiety management.

Munford, P. *Overcoming Compulsive Checking: Free Your Mind From OCD.*
Oakland: New Harbinger Publications, 2004.
This cognitive behavioral book specifically addresses compulsive checkers, dealing with eliminating or reducing obsessions, misspeaking, miswriting, or facing criticism or punishment for being at fault for fire, break-ins, flooding or injury to others.

Obsessive-Compulsive Anonymous: Recovering From Obsessive-Compulsive Disorder. New York: Alden Graphics Ltd., 1990.
The "Big Book" of OCA lays out the principles of this important 12-Step program of recovery.

Rapoport, J. *The Boy Who Couldn't Stop Washing.*
New York: Penguin Books, 1989.
The early classic that almost single-handedly brought OCD out of the closet—highly readable.

Roy C. *Obsessive-Compulsive Disorder: A Survival Guide for Family and Friends.*
New Hyde Park, NY: Obsessive Compulsive Anonymous, Inc., 1993.
One of the very first guides for the family—well-written and compassionately presented.

Schwartz, J. *Brain Lock: A Four-Step Self-Treatment Method to Change Your Brain Chemistry.* New York: HarperCollins Books, Inc., 1996.
A classic on the cognitive-behavioral treatment of OCD—strong dose of philosophy.

Stinnett, N. and DeFrain, J. *Secrets of Strong Families.* Boston: Little Brown and Company, 1985.
An excellent book, backed by research, describing what makes a family strong.

VanNoppen, B., Pato, M., and Rasmussen, S. *Learning to Live With OCD,* 4th Ed. OC Foundation: Milford, CN: 1997:
The latest edition, complete with the most up-to-date information, one of the first guides for healing the family by leading pioneers.

Woolis, R. *When Someone You Love Has a Mental Illness: A Handbook for Family, Friends, and Caregivers,* New York: Jeremy P. Tarcher/Putnam Books, 1992.
While written for families primarily under the influence of schizophrenia and the major mood disorders, this wonderful, practical guide can be used by families dealing with their loved ones with OCD.

Yaryura-Tobias, J. and Neziroglu, F. *Biobehavioral Treatment of Obsessive-Compulsive Spectrum Disorders.* New York: W.W. Norton & Company, 1997.
One of the best, short, all-around books providing an overview of OCD, even though it is somewhat technical.

Note: There are many excellent books, guides, pamphlets, and films—and I apologize in advance for any omissions.

—ᴍ—

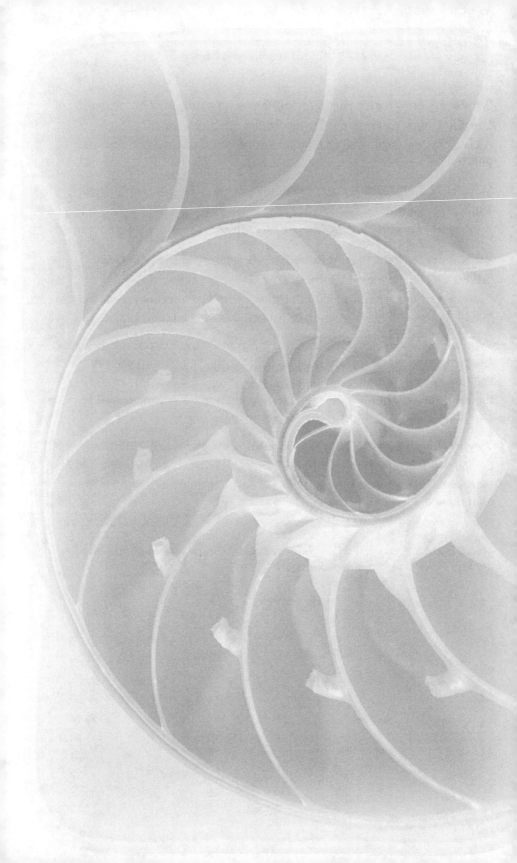

References

—⚉—

1. American Psychiatric Association. *Diagnostic and Statistical Manual of Mental Disorders* (4th ed.) Washington, D. C.: 1994.

2. Branden, N. *Taking Responsibility: Self-Reliance and the Accountable Life.* New York: Simon & Schuster, Inc., 1996.

3. Burland, J. *The Journey of Hope Family Education Course.* Poultney, VT: Alliance for the Mentally Ill of Vermont.

4. Burland, J. and Mayeux, D. *The Journey of Hope Family Support and Education Program,* 1996. Available through NAMI.

5. Beattie, M. *Co-dependent No More.* New York: Harper and Row, 1989.

6. C., Roy. *Obsessive-Compulsive Disorder: A Survival Guide for Family and Friends.* New Hyde Park, NY: Obsessive-Compulsive Anonymous, Inc., 1993.

7. Callahan, R. "Introduction of Thought Field Therapy." Callahan Techniques, Ltd. 619-345-9216, 1997.

8. Callner, J. "The Risk: A Story for Families About Courage, Hope and OCD." Awareness Films, 1995.

9. Callner, J. "The Touching Tree." Awareness Films, 1995.

10. Campbell, J. *The Hero With a Thousand Faces.* Princeton, NJ: Princeton University Press, 1968.

11. Carlson, R. and Shield, B. *Healers on Healing.* California: Jeremy P. Tarcher, Inc., 1989.

12. Cooper, M. *OCD and the Family.* An OC Foundation Video Presentation. Boston, MA: OC Foundation, 1995.

13. Cooper, M. "The Family's Involvement in OCD." *The Journal of the California Alliance for the Mentally Ill,* I, 17-18, 1995.

14. Covey, S. *The 7 Habits of Highly Effective Families.* Audio program, 1995.

15. Dubowski, C. "Living with Trichotillomania." *The Journal of the California Alliance for the Mentally Ill,* 1, 17-18, 1995.

16. Dumont, R. *The Sky Is Falling.* New York: W. W. Norton, 1995.

17. Erickson, M. and Rossi, E. *Hypnotherapy: An Exploratory Casebook.* New York: Irvington, 1979.

18. Figley, C. *Helping Traumatized Families.* San Francisco: Jossey-Bass, 1989.

19. Foa, E. and Wilson, R. *Stop Obsessing!* New York: Bantam, 1991.

20. Garfield, C. *Peak Performers: The New Heroes of American Business.* New York: Avon Books, 1986.

21. Greist, J. *Obsessive-Compulsive Disorder: A Guide.* Obsessive-Compulsive Information Center. Dean Foundation for Health, Research and Education, 1992.

22. Govig, S. D. *Souls Are Made of Endurance: Surviving Mental Illness in the Family.* Louisville, KY: Westminster John Knox Press, 1994.

23. Gravitz, H. L. "The Family as a Neglected Resource: Intergenerational Healing for Adult Children." *Trauma Response.* Fall, 1996.

24. Gravitz, H. L. "Intimates and Loved Ones: The Neglected Affected." *OCD Newsletter.* February, 1996.

25. Gravitz, H. L. "The Neglected Affected: Counseling the Codependents of OCD Sufferers." *Professional Counselor.* Oct., 1996. Vol. 11, No. 5.

26. Gravitz, H. L. *Trauma and Adversity: Triumph's Crucible.* (Forthcoming publication, 2006) Santa Barbara, CA: Healing Visions Press.

27. Gravitz, H. L. and Bowden, J .D. *Recovery: A Guide for Adult Children of Alcoholics*. New York: Simon & Schuster, 1987.

28. Harway, M. (Ed.) *Treating the Changing Family: Handling Normative and Unusual Events*. New York: John Wiley & Sons, Inc., 1996.

29. Hatfield, A. B. *A Family Education in Mental Illness*. New York: Guilford, 1990.

30. Hatfield, A. B. *Coping With Mental Illness in the Family: A Family Guide*. National Alliance for the Mentally Ill, 1991.

31. Houston, J. *The Search for the Beloved: Journey in Sacred Psychology*. Los Angeles: Jeremy P. Tarcher, Inc., 1987.

32. Jenike, M., Baer, L., and Minichiello, W. *Obsessive-Compulsive Disorder: Theory and Management*, 2nd Edition. St. Louis: Mosley Year Book, 1990.

33. Janoff-Bulman, R. *Shattered Assumptions: Towards a New Psychology of Trauma*. New York: The Free Press, 1992.

34. Johnston, H. and Fruehling, J. *Obsessive-Compulsive Disorder in Children and Adolescents: A Guide*. Paperback booklet, Madison, WI: Child Psychopharmacology Information Center, University of Wisconsin, 1997.

35. Johnson, J. *Hidden Victims. Hidden Healers. An Eight-Stage Healing Process for Families and Friends of the Mentally Ill*. Edina, MN: PEMA Publications, Inc., 1988.

36. Journal of Clinical Psychiatry. *The Expert Consensus Guideline Series: The Treatment of Obsessive-Compulsive Disorder*. Vol. 58, Supplement 4, 1997.

37. Katherine, A. Boundaries: *Where You End and I Begin*. New York: Simon & Schuster, 1996.

38. Kushner, H. *When Bad Things Happen to Good People*. New York: Avon Books, 1983.

39. Levine, S. *Healing Into Life and Death*. New York: Anchor Press/ Doubleday, 1987.

40. Livingston-VanNoppen, B., Rasmussen, S., and Eisen, J. (1990). "Family Function and Treatment in Obsesssive-Compulsive Disorder." In Jenike, M., Baer, L., & Minichiello, W. *Obsessive-Compulsive Disorders: Theory and Management*, 2nd Ed. St. Louis, MO: Mosby Year Book, 1990.

41. Marsh, D. *Families and Mental Illness: New Directions in Professional Practice.* New York: Praeger, 1992.

42. Marsh, D. and Dickens, R. *Troubled Journey: Coming to Terms With The Mental Illness of a Sibling or Parent.* New York: Tarcher/Putnam, 1997.

43. Moore, T. *Care of the Soul: A Guide for Cultivating Depth and Sacredness in Everyday Life.* New York: HarperCollins Publishers, Inc., 1992.

44. Myers, D. *The Pursuit of Happiness: Discovering the Pathway to Fulfillment, Well-Being, and Enduring Personal Joy.* New York: Avon Books, 1992.

45. *Obsessive-Compulsive Anonymous: Recovering From Obsessive-Compulsive Disorder.* New Hyde Park, New York: Obsessive-Compulsive Anonymous, Inc., 1990.

46. Pearsall, P. *Making Miracles.* New York: Simon & Schuster, Inc., 1991.

47. Peck, S. *The Road Less Traveled: A New Psychology of Love, Traditional Values and Spiritual Growth.* New York: Simon & Schuster, 1978.

48. Pipher, M. *The Shelter of Each Other.* New York: G. P. Putnam's Sons, 1996.

49. Rapoport, J. *The Boy Who Couldn't Stop Washing.* New York: Penguin Books, 1989.

50. Rasmussen, S. and Tsuang, M. "Epidemiology of Obsessive-Compulsive Disorder: A Review." *Journal of Clinical Psychiatry, 45,* 450-457, 1984.

51. Ross, J. *Triumph Over Fear.* New York: Bantam Books, 1994.

52. Schwartz, J. *Brain Lock: A Four-Step Self-Treatment Method to Change Your Brain Chemistry.* New York: HarperCollins Books, Inc., 1996.

53. Shapiro, F. *Eye Movement Desensitization and Reprocessing: Basic Principles, Protocols, and Procedures.* New York: The Guilford Press, 1995.

54. Shapiro, F. and Forrest, M. *EMDR: The Breakthrough Therapy for Overcoming Anxiety, Stress, and Trauma.* New York: HarperCollins Publishers, Inc., 1997.

55. Stearns, A. *Coming Back: Rebuilding Lives After Crisis and Loss.* New York: Random House, 1988.

56. Steketee, G. and White, K. *When Once Is Not Enough.* Oakland, CA: New Harbinger Publications, Inc., 1990.

57. Stinnett, N. and DeFrain, J. *Secrets of Strong Families.* Boston: Little Brown and Company, 1985.

58. Strong, M. *Mainstay: For the Well Spouse of the Chronically Ill.* New York: Penguin Books, 1988.

59. VanNoppen, B., Pato, M. and Rasmussen, S. *Learning to Live With OCD,* 4th ed. OC Foundation: Milford, CT, 1997.

60. Van der Kolk, B. *Psychological Trauma.* Washington, D. C.: American Psychiatric Press, 1986.

61. Woolis, Rebecca. *When Someone You Love Has a Mental Illness: A Handbook for Family, Friends, and Caregivers.* New York: Putnam Publishing Group, 1992.

62. Yaryura-Tobias, J. and Neziroglu, F. *Biobehavioral Treatment of Obsessive-Compulsive Spectrum Disorders.* New York: W. W. Norton & Company, 1997.

63. Zohar, D. *The Quantum Self: Human Nature and Consciousness Defined by the New Physics.* New York: Quick/William Morrow, 1990.

—⚬⚬—

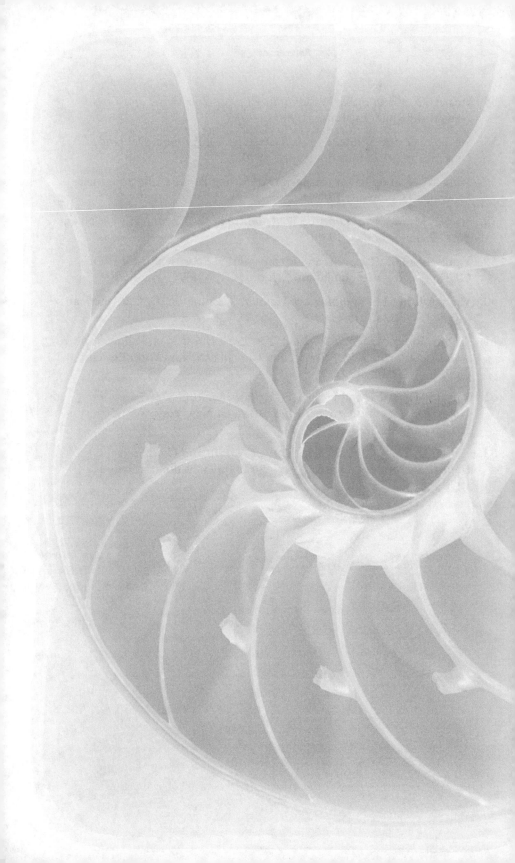

About the Author

—∿—

Herbert L. Gravitz, Ph.D., received his Master's Degree and Doctor of Philosophy in psychology from the University of Tennessee in 1969. A licensed psychologist, his private practice in clinical psychology is located in Santa Barbara, California. He specializes in the diagnosis and treatment of the effects of illness, addiction, and other trauma on the individual, the family, and society. He is known for his innovative work in systemic traumatology, specifically the impact of alcoholism, post-traumatic stress disorder (PTSD), obsessive-compulsive disorder (OCD), bipolar disorder, major depression, and schizophrenia on the individual and the whole family.

Dr. Gravitz has authored or co-authored books and articles on trauma, healing, and recovery, and he has led workshops and seminars throughout the United States on the traumatic impact of alcoholism and major mental illness on the family. He is the co-author of *Recovery: A Guide for Adult Children of Alcoholics,* a modern classic in the field of children of alcoholics, and he is co-author of *Genesis: Spirituality in Recovery from Childhood Traumas.* He authored *Mental Illness and the Family: Unlocking the Doors to Triumph,* which has received endorsements from professionals and organizations, as well as individuals and their families. He recently finished *Facing Adversity: Words That Heal,* the companion book for *Unlocking the Doors to Triumph,* and is currently completing a new book, titled *Trauma and Adversity: Triumph's Crucible,* in which he shares in depth his pioneering synthesis of the fields of trauma, addiction, loss and grief, altered states of consciousness, physical healing, mythology, personal excellence, the new sciences, the energy therapies, and spirituality, all of which lead to a powerful healing transformation. His Web site is www.HealTheFamily.com and his e-mail address is mail@HealTheFamily.com.

Dr. Gravitz' message of hope and optimism regarding the impact of illness, addiction, and trauma on both the individual and the family makes him a frequent guest on radio and television. In addition to his busy private practice in Santa Barbara, he is a Founding Member of the Board of Directors of the National Association of Children of Alcoholics (NACoA) and served on its Advisory Board. He is also a Founding Member of the Board of Directors of The Memory to Action Project, a not-for-profit organization whose mission is to commemorate genocide, encourage tolerance, and promote commitment to social action. He holds Diplomates in Psychotherapy, Traumatic Stress, and Forensic Psychology. In addition, he is Board Certified in Illness Trauma by the American Academy of Experts in Traumatic Stress.

Dr. Gravitz' first experience with people suffering from mental illness occurred following his first year of graduate school, when he worked as a psychiatric aide at Chestnut Lodge, an internationally known residential treatment center in Rockville, Maryland. He did his clinical internship at Larue D. Carter Memorial Hospital in Indianapolis, Indiana, in 1968, where he worked with the seriously mentally ill in an in-patient setting. From 1972 to 1980, while first Assistant Director and later Program Director of the University of California at Santa Barbara Counseling Center, he worked extensively with students who experienced serious mental illness. When he entered private practice in 1980, he counseled the seriously mentally ill and their families in his role as Psychological Consultant to Sanctuary House. Sanctuary House was started as an alternative residential treatment program for the seriously mentally ill, and it became a nationally respected treatment facility that continues to serve the needs of the mentally ill and their families. While at Sanctuary House, he formed the first group psychotherapy program for its residents and frequently consulted with family members. In 1983, he served as a consultant to the Santa Barbara Psychiatric Emergency Team where he provided staff development.

It was not until the early 1990s that Dr. Gravitz became aware of how many clients in his outpatient private practice also were the family members of those who suffered from serious mental illnesses, such as schizophrenia, bipolar disorder, major depression, obsessive-compulsive disorder, or some other severe illness. By the middle of the 1990s, he began to describe the plight of the family that was living under the influence of mental illness.

Because illness, addiction, and trauma often occur together in the same family, Dr. Gravitz has learned to address all three in unique ways that go beyond traditional family approaches. In this process, he has discovered ways to speak simultaneously to the sufferer and to the sufferer's loved ones. Dr. Gravitz routinely began to treat the family as a whole in the late 1990s, regardless of how many family members were actually present in a session. He continues to forge new frontiers in his intensive and creative consultations. In this regard, he is known for his innovative intergenerational treatment protocols and his pioneering work in "untimed" consultation sessions, in which the family works on an issue until everyone present agrees it is time to stop.

—◊◊◊—

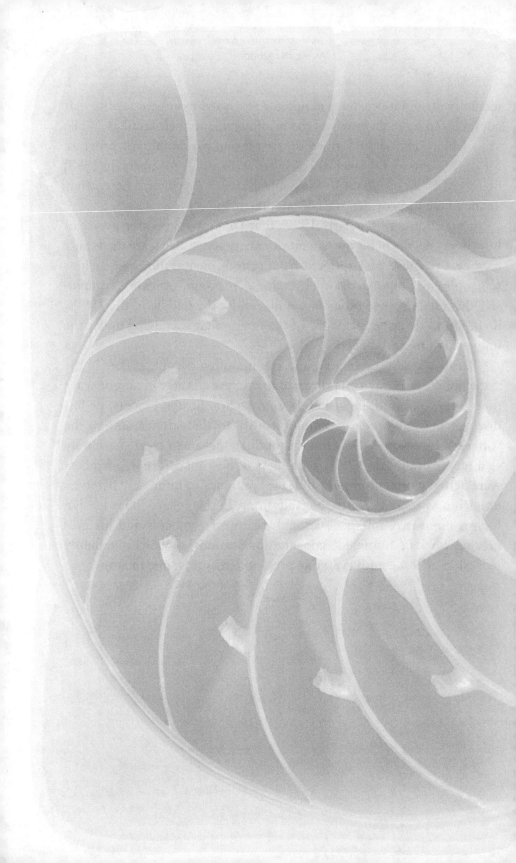

Share Your Story

—✺—

In preparation for the next edition of *Obsessive-Compulsive Disorder: New Help for the Family*, I will continue to gather information on family healing and recovery. Now that you have finished reading this book, I invite you to share a personal account of how OCD has affected your family. I am especially looking for reports of how you and your family have been able to use the principles and skills described in this book.

While the numbers may be few, there are accounts of families experiencing love and satisfaction even in the midst of OCD. Perhaps you have a story or even a poem that describes how you and your family have dealt effectively with OCD. If so, please send your story or poem to me at the following address.

Dr. Herbert L. Gravitz
Healing Visions Press • P.O. Box 4035 • San Luis Obispo, CA 93403

Or e-mail: info@HealTheFamily.com

I will credit you if you wish, or your anonymity will be honored if so desired. Thank you in advance for your help.

Quick Order Form

Online orders	www.HealTheFamily.com
Fax orders	805-543-5160
Telephone orders	800-718-7080 or 805-545-8398
E-mail orders	orders@HealTheFamily.com
Postal orders	Healing Visions Press
	P.O. Box 4035
	San Luis Obispo, CA 93403

I would like to order additional copies of *Obsessive-Compulsive Disorder: New Help for the Family, Second Edition* at $21.95 each. (See below.)

For quantity discounts and special sales, please go to orders@HealTheFamily.com or call 800-718-7080.

If you found this book helpful, you might be interested in the following from Healing Visions Press

Quantity	**Item**	**Total Price**
_____	*Obsessive-Compulsive Disorder: New Help for the Family, Second Edition* @$21.95	_____
_____	*Mental Illness and the Family: Unlocking the Doors to Triumph* @$24.95	_____
_____	*Facing Adversity: Words That Heal* @$24.95	_____

Sales tax: _____

(Please add 7.75% for books shipped to CA addresses)

Shipping & handling: _____

($5.00 for the first book and $3.00 for each additional book)

Total Due: _____

Name _____

Address _____

City _____

State _____ Zip _____

Telephone: _____ E-Mail address: _____

Payment____Check *(Make checks payable to Healing Visions Press)*

____Visa ____MasterCard

Card number: _____

Name on card _____ Exp. Date _____

Thank you for your order!
Please visit our website at www.HealTheFamily.com